ABOUT THE A

Aidan Dunlea BComm ACA is Finance Manager for Murphy's Brewery Ireland and was formerly a general practice manager with a Big Six firm.

Niall MacLochlainn BComm FCA is company secretary and financial manager for Mitsui Denman (Ireland) Limited. He has lectured in financial and management accounting to students taking their final professional accounting examinations and is a past Secretary of both the Cork and Munster Societies of Chartered Accountants.

AUDITING STANDARDS

A Quick Reference

Second Edition

Aidan Dunlea and
Niall MacLochlainn

Oak Tree Press
Dublin • London

Oak Tree Press
Merrion Building,
Lower Merrion Street,
Dublin 2

http://www.oaktreepress.com

A catalogue record for this book is
available from the British Library.

ISBN 1-86076-087-2

Second edition
First edition published 1995

Printed in Ireland by Colour Books, Dublin.

CONTENTS

Accounting Systems and Internal Control

Evidence

Using the Work of Others

Reporting

STATEMENTS OF INVESTMENT CIRCULAR
REPORTING STANDARDS

INTRODUCTION TO SECOND EDITION

This book is intended as a companion volume to *Accounting Standards: A Quick Reference* (now in its third edition) and has been developed with the same objectives in mind. Students of auditing will find it useful as an initial introduction to auditing standards, as well as a convenient means of revising the great bulk of material they contain. Practitioners, especially those in smaller practices, will find it useful as a means of updating their knowledge on the many recent developments in auditing. We hope that the Application Notes will prove useful to practitioners in implementing the key points required by the standards.

As a result of comments about the first edition, we have expanded the contents to include brief outlines of Statements of Investment Circular Reporting Standards, Practice Notes, Bulletins, Discussion Papers and proposed standards in issue at 16 January 1998.

The contents are up-to-date at the time of going to press and, because auditing standards are continually developing, further editions will be published from time to time to ensure that readers are kept abreast of developments.

Our aim — as suggested by the title — is to provide a quick and easy work of reference, one we hope that readers will find both comprehensive and concise. Your comments and suggestions on how we might improve the book for its users are welcome.

Aidan Dunlea
Niall MacLochlainn
January 1998

THE DEVELOPMENT OF AUDITING STANDARDS

The development of formal auditing standards and guidelines began with the formation of the Auditing Practices Committee (APC) in 1976.

Auditing Practices Committee

APC was established by the Consultative Committee of Accountancy Bodies (CCAB), which comprises the six principal accountancy bodies in the United Kingdom and Ireland:

- The Association of Chartered Certified Accountants (ACCA)

- The Chartered Institute of Management Accountants (CIMA)

- The Chartered Institute of Public Finance and Accountancy (CIPFA)

- The Institute of Chartered Accountants in England and Wales (ICAEW)

- The Institute of Chartered Accountants in Ireland (ICAI)

- The Institute of Chartered Accountants of Scotland (ICAS).

APC developed almost 50 pronouncements relating to the audit of entities, covering topics as diverse as:

- Reporting to shareholders and management

- Procedures to be undertaken in specific circumstances

- Guidance for particular sectors and industries and in operational circumstances.

Throughout, the basis of the auditor's work was the statutory duty set out in company law.

Auditing Practices Board

Because of rapid changes in the business world and the increasing demands of users of financial statements, a new body, the Auditing Practices Board (APB), was set up in 1991 by CCAB. This new board differs from its predecessor in that its voting membership is evenly divided between practising auditors and user representatives (including nominees of the Bank of England, the London Stock Exchange, the National Audit Office, the Audit Commission, the Securities and Investments Board, the UK Department of Trade and Industry, and the Irish Department of Enterprise, Trade and Employment).

Towards the end of 1997, it was proposed that a new independent foundation and review board be established and that APB should be transferred from the CCAB to this foundation, subject to review after three years. At the time of going to press, this proposal had not been acted on.

APB's stated objectives are:

- To establish high standards in auditing

- To meet the developing needs of users of financial information

- To ensure there is public confidence in the audit process.

The concerns and perceptions of the auditing process as expressed by a (limited) survey of users of financial statements was set out in APB's paper *The Future Development of Auditing* (November 1992) and included:

- **Role and scope of the audit**: Auditors should also recognise that there are other interest groups — not just shareholders. Auditors should be concerned with directors' stewardship, future prospects and risks (not just the historical aspect of financial statements), detection of fraud and the effectiveness of internal controls.

- **Independence**: A perception that auditors are not sufficiently independent.

- **Audit report**: A perception that audit reports are not informative enough, do not set out major findings, or issues or concerns raised during the audit.

- **Competition**: Concern that audit standards may have been lowered in order to match competitors' (lower) fees.

- **Litigation**: Well-publicised legal cases against auditors act as a barrier to audit innovation.

- **Regulation**: A perception that the audit regulation system was not effective. (It was not clear to APB whether those surveyed were aware of the changes recently made on the implementation of the EU Eighth Directive — see section on the legal framework for the new rules).

- **Skills**: A greater need for continuous training and development of auditors (to meet the changing needs of users).

Future Developments

Following consultation on the 1992 paper, APB issued *The Audit Agenda* (December 1994) and, following responses, a further document, *The Audit Agenda — The Next Steps*, was issued in February 1996. These propose a framework for the future development of auditing. A summary of *The Audit Agenda — Next Steps* appears on page 192.

Pronouncements

APB's pronouncements fall into three main categories:

- Statements of Auditing Standards (SASs)
- Practice Notes
- Bulletins.

There are also Statements of Investment Circular Reporting Standards (SIRs), a Statement on Audit Exemption Reports, consultative documents, research documents and other documents of general interest issued on both auditing and related services.

Proposed auditing standards are issued in draft form for comment and sometimes reissued again as a draft in the light of the arguments expressed. Before a draft statement becomes a full standard, it must be approved by at least 75 per cent of the voting members of APB.

Compliance

Compliance with the basic principles and essential procedures in SASs is mandatory for all auditors. Explanatory and other material in the standards provide an aid to interpretation.

Practice Notes, Bulletins, consultative documents and research documents indicate APB's view of the correct procedures to be followed but are not mandatory. SASs use words like plan, design, assess, consider. In practice, the auditor must decide, using his or her professional judgement, the meaning of these words as they relate to each client. In the event of litigation, the auditor must be able to justify the original judgement. Good documentation (a requirement of the standards) is clearly imperative!

Effective date for implementation of auditing standards

Most of the auditing standards (SASs) came into effect for audits of financial statements for periods ending on or after 23 December 1995.

The effective dates for the others were:

SAS 100 .... 30 June 1995

SAS 120 .... 30 June 1995

SAS 130 .... 30 June 1995

SAS 600 .... 30 September 1993

SAS 620 .... 1 May 1994.

AUDITING — THE LEGAL FRAMEWORK

The Eighth Directive of the European Community (now the European Union) was enacted into UK law by the 1989 Companies Act (in Ireland, by the 1990 Companies Act).

As a result, the law now sets out specific rules on the following matters:

- Qualification for appointment as auditor
- Resignation of an auditor
- Removal of an auditor
- Registration of auditors
- Auditors' rights (and duties) relating to books of account
- Auditors' rights to attend and be heard at general meetings
- Penalties for making false statements to auditors.

Qualification for appointment as auditor

To qualify as an auditor, an individual must be a member of one of the Recognised Supervisory Bodies (RSBs) and be eligible under its rules to practice as an auditor.

In the case of a partnership or incorporated practice, the individuals responsible for the conduct of audit work ("responsible individuals") must be qualified members of an RSB. Where the partnership contains unqualified partners, these persons must become affiliates or regulated non-members of the RSB. Control of the partnership (75 per cent of voting rights) must be held by qualified individuals or registered auditors.

In the UK, the RSBs are recognised by order of the Department of Trade and Industry or the Department of

Economic Development (Northern Ireland). In Ireland,
RSBs are recognised by the Department of Enterprise,
Trade and Employment.

To be recognised as an RSB, a body must have rules
to ensure that its members:

• Conduct their work with professional integrity

• Comply with technical standards

• Remain competent

• Are independent of their clients.

In addition, an RSB must have provisions relating to
disciplinary procedures — that is, investigation of com-
plaints against members, admission and expulsion of
members, suspension, or withdrawal of practising certificate etc.

The legislation also specifies those who are ineligible
to act as auditors. These are persons closely connected
with the audited entity, such as:

• An officer or servant

• A person who was an officer or servant within the
  period to which the audit related

• A close relation of an officer

• A partner of, or someone employed by, an officer

• A person disqualified as auditor of a group company.

Note: A body corporate is not permitted to conduct
audits of companies registered under legislation in the
Republic of Ireland.

Resignation of an Auditor

If an auditor of a limited company wishes to resign, or does not wish to be re-appointed, he or she must:

- Notify the company in writing

- Include a statement that there are no circumstances which he or she believes should be brought to the notice of the members or creditors of the company

- Send a copy of the notice to the company (in Ireland, he or she must also notify the Registrar of Companies within 14 days).

If there are circumstances that the auditor believes should be brought to the notice of members or creditors in relation to his/her resignation, the company must:

- Send a copy of the auditor's notice to every person entitled to receive a copy of the accounts

- Convene an extraordinary general meeting, if requested by the auditor

- Circulate a further statement from the auditor regarding the circumstances connected with the resignation, if requested.

Removal of an Auditor

Extended notice (28 days, instead of the normal 21 days for an ordinary resolution) is required where a limited company proposes to remove an auditor, or to appoint another instead, at the AGM.

The company must notify the present auditor, who is entitled to attend and be heard at the general meeting on any part of the business that concerns him as former auditor.

Registration of Auditors

Details of all those qualified for appointment as auditor
are available for public inspection. In the UK, the list is
maintained by the RSBs; in Ireland, the list is available
for inspection at the Companies Registration Office,
Dublin Castle.

Auditor's Rights (and Duties) Relating to Books of Account

The auditor is entitled to:

* Right of access at all reasonable times to the books,
  accounts and vouchers of the company

* Request any employee of the company for such information and explanations considered necessary for
  the performance of the duties of the audit

* Request information from subsidiary companies and
  their auditors.

If an auditor forms an opinion, at any time, that proper
books of account are not being kept by the company, he
or she must serve notice on the entity stating his or her
opinion (and, if the position is not rectified within seven
days, must notify the Registrar of Companies).

Auditor's Rights Relating to General Meetings

The auditor:

* Is entitled to receive all notices of all general meetings

* Is entitled to be heard at the meetings

* Must read the auditors' report at annual general
  meetings of the company.

Penalties for Making False Statements to Auditors

It is a criminal offence for an employee of a company to knowingly or recklessly give a misleading, false or deceptive statement to an auditor.

STATEMENTS OF AUDITING STANDARDS
(AT 1 JANUARY 1998)

Introductory Matters

Responsibility

Planning, Controlling and Recording

Accounting Systems and Internal Control

Evidence

Using the Work of Others

Reporting

SAS 010

THE SCOPE AND AUTHORITY OF APB PRONOUNCEMENTS

ISSUED MAY 1993

Summary

Sets out the principal categories of pronouncements of the Auditing Practices Board (APB), the distinctions between them, and the authority of each.

Key Points

Pronouncements of the APB include:

* Statements of Auditing Standards (SASs)
* Practice Notes
* Bulletins
* Other documents

SASs

Auditors must comply with Basic Principles when auditing financial statements (mandatory).

Only apply SASs to material items.

SASs include explanatory and other material to assist interpretation of basic principles (this material is not mandatory).

Apparent failure to comply with SASs could result in disciplinary or regulatory action being taken against an auditor (practising certificate could be suspended or re-voked).

SASs are likely to be used in a court of law as evidence of the standard of work required of an auditor.

SASs comply, where possible, with equivalent standards set out by the International Auditing Practices Committee.

Practice Notes

These set out how to apply SASs to particular circumstances and/or industries (persuasive but not mandatory).

Bulletins

Guidance on new or emerging issues (persuasive but not mandatory).

Other documents

Consultative documents, research studies etc. issued to stimulate debate and interest in the auditing process.

Note: Since the publication of SAS 010, the APB has also issued:

• Statements of Standards for Reporting Accountants — audit exemption reports

• Statements of Investment Circular Reporting Standards.

These are summarised later in this book.

SAS 100

OBJECTIVE AND GENERAL PRINCIPLES GOVERNING AN AUDIT OF FINANCIAL STATEMENTS

ISSUED MARCH 1995

Summary

Sets out the objectives and principles governing audits of financial statements.

Key Points

Auditors must:

- Comply with auditing standards as set out in Statements of Auditing Standards (SASs)

- Design procedures to obtain sufficient evidence that financial statements:

  ◊ Contain no material misstatement

  ◊ Are prepared in accordance with accounting standards and company law

- Issue an audit report setting out a clear opinion

- Comply with ethical principles (integrity; objectivity; independence; professional competence and behaviour; confidentiality).

The management of an entity is responsible for the preparation and presentation of financial statements.

Application Notes

Inform client in writing (prior to commencement of the audit) of the basis of fees charged for the services provided.

Ensure that the client has full and complete understanding of:

- Services to be covered by the fee

- Basis of fees charged for present and for future years (important when competitive quote is requested).

Be able to demonstrate that SASs were followed and that the client understands the fee basis if a very low fee level is quoted.

Auditors may exercise a lien on certain books and papers of a client in respect of unpaid fees. However, the auditor should take reasonable steps to resolve any such dispute before exercising a lien.

Regularly review the ethical guidelines set out by the relevant RSB and ensure compliance with same.

Regularly review the guidelines on maintaining competence (recruitment, training policies) issued by the RSBs.

Design procedures to ensure that all audits are conducted in accordance with SASs. Monitor compliance with audit regulations (termed "internal monitoring"/"quality assurance"/"audit compliance") on a regular basis — sample audit files annually.

Design procedures to ensure that all financial statements are prepared in accordance with relevant financial reporting standards and legislation.

SAS 110

FRAUD AND ERROR

ISSUED JANUARY 1995

Summary

Sets out standards required of, and gives guidance to, auditors when considering the possibility of fraud and/or error in financial statements.

Key Points

Directors have a responsibility to prevent and detect fraud or error by developing proper accounting and internal control systems.

Auditors must assess the risk of material errors in the financial statements due to fraud or unintentional mistakes.

Design audit procedures to reasonably detect material misstatements in the financial statements.

Fraud is often difficult to detect. If misstatement is suspected, perform additional procedures. Document the nature, circumstances and possible effect of suspected fraud or error.

If a suspicion of error persists, discuss it with (the appropriate level of) management, directors or audit committee.

If a material error is found, disclose it immediately to management, the board of directors, or audit committee.

Consider the implications of the material error on the accounts, management representations, other audit procedures performed and the audit report.

Auditors may have to report suspected cases of fraud (or error) to third parties by law (refer to SAS 620) or in "public interest cases" (because of potential breach of confidentiality, which can only be justified in exceptional circumstances, auditors should obtain legal advice to ensure that qualified privilege is retained).

The requirements of this SAS apply to all activities of the entity — including those carried on abroad.

Application Notes

At the audit planning stage, consider whether any of the following circumstances apply (which increase the risk of error) and plan the audit accordingly:

- Competence of management is in query

- Failure in internal controls

- High turnover of key accounting personnel

- Major understaffing in the finance department

- Pressures within the operation (for example, short life products needing major investment; changes in customer mix or their credit terms; lack of working capital; very severe accounting deadlines)

- Unusual transactions, especially near the year end, that have a major impact on the results

- Where sufficient audit evidence is not obtained or is difficult to obtain

- Transactions with related parties

- Management has not acted on weaknesses in internal control pointed out in previous management letters.

Discuss with management the procedures in place for detecting and preventing fraud or error. Suggest improvements if weaknesses are noted.

Ensure the letter of engagement establishes the responsibility of management to prevent and detect fraud and error.

In a group situation, ensure that auditors of subsidiaries (including foreign components) conduct their audits in accordance with this SAS.

Where audit procedures indicate the likely occurrence of fraud or error, perform additional or modified audit procedures. Report instances of fraud or error to management, directors or audit committee (as appropriate).

Consider the implications of fraud or error detected during the audit, particularly on the validity of management representations.

If fraud or error is detected, ensure it is properly disclosed and/or accounted for in the financial statements. Even if corrected, it may be necessary to qualify the audit report.

Consider the need for legal advice if fraud or error is detected. In extreme cases, there may be a need to make disclosure to a proper authority. Consider the conflict between client confidentiality and public interest.

Obtain written confirmation from directors that the financial statements contain no material misstatements caused by fraud or error.

In exceptional cases, consider withdrawal from audit engagement.

Definitions

Fraud
The use of deception to obtain an unjust or illegal financial advantage, or intentional misrepresentations.

Error
An unintentional mistake in financial statements.

SAS 120

CONSIDERATION OF LAW AND REGULATIONS

ISSUED JANUARY 1995

Summary

Sets out the responsibility of auditors to consider the effect on the financial statements of non-compliance with the laws and regulations applicable to an entity.

Key Points

Directors are responsible for compliance with the various laws and regulations affecting the business, both in the home market and abroad.

Auditors must ensure that the financial statements are prepared in conformity with the relevant laws and regulations (primary responsibility).

Auditors must obtain a general understanding of the statutory framework of the business operations. Develop procedures for this.

Obtain from the directors written confirmation of all possible non-compliance, including the consequences of same. Read correspondence between the entity and the appropriate authorities. If there is no non-compliance, the auditor need not investigate further.

If non-compliance is admitted by the directors or becomes known during the audit, discuss it with the directors. Reconsider (if appropriate) the assessment of audit risk and the reliability of audit evidence.

Auditors have a responsibility to qualify their report to shareholders if non-compliance has had a material effect on the financial statements (where there is incorrect accounting treatment or inadequate disclosure).

In certain cases, auditors may have to report non-compliance to third parties (for example, regulatory authorities).

Application Notes

For each client, list (in the permanent audit file) the particular laws and regulations applicable to the entity. These may apply to the entity as a whole, or to certain sections or products. Update this list each year.

Keep an abstract of the key regulations. Confirm each year that no change has occurred (amend if applicable).

Ensure that management understands its obligation to comply with laws and regulations governing both the preparation of financial statements and the environment within which the entity conducts its business. Include a note to this effect in the engagement letter.

Check:

- Whether the client has procedures to ensure that new regulations are notified to those responsible in the entity

- Whether the client has procedures for monitoring compliance with laws and reporting breaches of regulations

- What action has been taken when breaches in regulations were reported previously.

Read the correspondence files between the entity and the appropriate authorities. Consider whether a letter directly from the relevant authority is required to confirm the situation.

Ensure that the audit team is aware of any statutory requirement to report the entity's compliance with specific laws or regulations to a third party (see SAS 620).

In the letter of representation, obtain confirmation from the directors that they have disclosed all possible non-compliance, and actual or contingent consequences arising therefrom.

Consider the impact of any non-compliance on audit risk and the validity of management representations.

Report instances of non-compliance to management, directors or audit committee, as appropriate.

Report instances of material non-compliance to the addressees of audit report (see SAS 600).

Consider the need to disclose any breaches in compliance to the proper authority in the public interest. Obtain legal advice before doing so, if necessary.

In a group situation, ensure that the auditors of subsidiaries (including foreign components) also apply appropriate procedures.

In exceptional cases, consider withdrawal from the audit engagement.

Comment

With many new EU directives being issued each year, it is important that the client (and the auditor) has procedures in place to learn about new legislation. Some legislation is of general application — for example, health and safety (VDUs, manual handling, product liability and packaging waste) — but some is specific to one industry — for example, the requirement for hauliers to comply with the regulations governing the carriage of dangerous goods by road.

SAS 130

THE GOING CONCERN BASIS IN FINANCIAL STATEMENTS

ISSUED NOVEMBER 1994

Summary

Sets out standards for auditors in assessing whether the going concern concept should be used (and the basis adequately disclosed) in the financial statements.

Key Points

Applies to all audits intended to give a true and fair view.

The directors must satisfy themselves, by considering the entity's future, that the going concern concept is appropriate in preparing the financial statements and that the Notes to the financial statements contain relevant disclosures where necessary.

Where the directors do not attempt to satisfy themselves adequately, this constitutes a limitation of audit scope.

The auditor must plan the audit and design audit procedures to identify material matters in the period that directors have considered that could impact on the going concern concept.

The future period for assessing going concern is not specified — and will thus depend on each entity's circumstances — but a guideline of one year from the accounts approval date is indicated.

If a short period (less than one year ahead) is chosen by the directors, they will have to decide whether to include additional disclosures explaining the assumptions in the financial statements. The auditor must consider whether these disclosures are adequate.

If the directors' disclosures are not adequate, include the necessary further disclosures as part of the audit opinion (qualification of the audit opinion is not required on the basis of non-disclosure alone).

If the auditor has a significant worry about the appropriateness of the going concern basis, include an explanatory paragraph in the audit report but do not qualify.

The auditor must discuss with the directors the future viability of the entity and consider whether written representations from the directors are required.

If written representations are requested and not given, consider:

- Why representations were not given

- Whether this constitutes a limitation on audit scope (if so, qualify audit opinion).

If the auditor disagrees that the going concern basis is appropriate, he or she should give an adverse audit opinion. Inform the directors that they should obtain legal advice on the implications of trading while the entity is (or may be) insolvent.

Examine cash flow forecasts, the extent of borrowing facilities, the amount and pattern of supplier credit, and the directors' plans for the business (look at key as-

sumptions used, apply sensitivity analysis, and assess
bankers' intentions regarding facilities). Discussion with
the directors regarding future plans may be sufficient to
satisfy the auditor that a period of one year from the accounts approval date has been examined by the directors
in assessing the appropriateness of the going concern
basis.

Apply SAS 130 to group accounts, even though one or
more subsidiaries' accounts may not be prepared on a
going concern basis.

Application Notes

At the audit planning stage, perform a preliminary assessment of the appropriateness of the going concern
basis for the preparation of financial statements — discuss with the directors.

Consider the period chosen by the directors in assessing
whether the entity is a going concern — is it reasonable
and does it have regard to the foreseeable future?

Check whether management has systems in place to
identify future uncertainties affecting going concern (for
example, projected sales, profits, cash flow statements).
Suggest improvements if weaknesses are noted.

Consider whether any of the following apply:

- Substantial sales of fixed assets (not being replaced)
- Major restructuring of debt
- Legal restrictions on operations (in any market)
- Obsolescence of a key product due to technology

- Loss of major customers, suppliers, or management staff

- Depressed markets, where the company is heavily dependent on a few products

- Excess of liabilities over assets

- Cash flow problems — inability to pay creditors on due dates/difficulties in keeping within bank facility limits

- Defaults on loan agreements

- Significant operating losses

- Shortage of important supplies, or labour difficulties.

This list is not all-inclusive, nor does the existence of one or more of the above always signify a going concern issue. Other factors may lessen the significance of these indicators.

Review cash flow, results and other forecasts for at least one year (normally) from audit completion date. Examine significant assumptions for reasonableness.

If the directors have chosen a period of less than one year from approval date of the financial statements for the assessment of going concern, perform the above tests for the period and ensure the reasons for the choice of period are given in the financial statements.

In a smaller entity, discussion with directors regarding future plans and information relating to business trends may be sufficient — summarise the discussions.

Audit staff should immediately report any matters indicating going concern difficulties to the audit partner for discussion with the directors.

Consider the implications of going concern matters for the financial statements, including situations where another basis of accounting has been used.

Ensure that appropriate references to matters that may impact on the going concern basis are included in the letter of representation (which should be dated as close as possible to the date of signing the audit report).

In a group situation, consider whether the qualification of a subsidiary's accounts on a going concern basis has an impact on the consolidated statements.

SAS 140

ENGAGEMENT LETTERS

ISSUED MARCH 1995

Summary

Sets out requirements for engagement letters — both the content of a letter and its communication to the client.

Key Points

Auditors should agree in writing the terms of the engagement with each new client.

SAS applies also to other services such as tax, accounting, management consultancy.

Update the engagement letter where necessary (if not necessary, remind client of the original letter) — for example, where there is new management, new owners, or a change of business.

If asked to change the terms of the engagement before it is completed:

- If appropriate, update the engagement letter
- If not appropriate, consider position — take legal advice, if necessary.

Application Notes

Issue an engagement letter to each audit client.

Reissue the engagement letter at least every three years.

Revise the engagement letter immediately each time there is a major change in key personnel, new directors, owners, or in client's business.

Confirm the terms of engagement annually with client when a new letter is not issued.

Tailor the engagement letter for each client's circumstances, requirements, etc. (although they will have common headings).

Issue a separate engagement letter where services other than audit (for example, taxation, accounting, investment business advice, etc.) are being given.

In joint audits, confirm the respective responsibilities of the participating firms and issue a joint letter of engagement. Consider the need for separate engagement letters for subsidiaries or other segments of the entity.

Contents of engagement letters

An engagement letter should include:

- Summary of responsibilities of directors and auditors
- Scope of the engagement
- Form of any reports
- Confirmation of acceptance by the auditor
- Fees, billing — agreed fee and payment terms (or basis of billing)

- Reference to other engagements between auditor and client

- Timetable for the engagement

- Involvement of internal auditors, other auditors or experts

- A list of the work the client is to do and expected date of completion

- A request for details of stocktaking arrangements, locations, times, etc.

- Procedures to be followed in the event of complaint (required automatically by some professional bodies).

The statement of responsibilities of the directors should refer to:

- Preparation of financial statements which give a true and fair view

- Keeping proper accounting records and safeguarding the assets of the entity (statutory duties)

- Preventing and detecting fraud and error (SAS 110)

- Compliance with laws and regulations affecting the entity (SAS 120)

- Selecting suitable accounting policies and applying them consistently

- Making estimates and judgements that are reasonable and prudent

- Preparation of financial statements on a going concern basis — unless it is not appropriate (SAS 130)

- Giving all information and explanations required by the auditors, including events post balance sheet.

SAS 150

SUBSEQUENT EVENTS

ISSUED MARCH 1995

Summary

Sets out the standards required in assessing the impact of events occurring after the balance sheet date up to the time the financial statements are put before the members for approval.

Key Points

Three stages to be considered:

- From the end of the accounting period to the date of the audit report

- From the date of the audit report to the issue of the financial statements

- After the financial statements have been issued but before they are laid before the members.

Stage 1

Design audit procedures to ensure that all material post balance sheet events to the date of the audit report are treated correctly in the financial statements (refer to SSAP 17 *Post Balance Sheet Events*).

Stage 2

There is no responsibility to perform audit procedures or make enquiries. But if the auditor becomes aware of material events affecting the financial statements, the choices are:

- To issue a new audit report on amended financial statements

- To issue a qualified report (assuming none issued to date), where the directors do not amend the financial statements

- To request management not to issue financial statements to members (or anyone else). If financial statements are issued, the auditor should consider making a statement at the entity's AGM and also consider their position as auditor.

Stage 3

There is no responsibility on the auditor to make enquiries. But if the auditor becomes aware of material events which, if known during the audit, might have resulted in a different audit report, he or she should discuss them with the directors and consider the implications.

If amended financial statements are issued, a new audit report is required. This must:

- Include an explanatory paragraph regarding the change (or refer to a new Note in the financial statements which should set out the reason)

- Refer to the earlier report

- Be newly dated.

Ensure that management informs those who received a copy of earlier financial statements of the new situation.

Application Notes

Perform the review of subsequent events as near as possible to the date of signing the audit report.

Review minutes of meetings of directors, management, audit committee, etc. post year-end.

Compare actual results for the new financial year against budget. Make enquiries, if major variances are arising.

Note details of any new financing arranged, the outcome of review of banking facilities, etc.   SAs 130

Review the cash flow post year-end. Note any unusual payments or receipts.

Arrange for auditors of other subsidiaries or associates of the entity to notify the principal auditor of important issues affecting their audit.

While discussing the final draft of the accounts, enquire of management whether any subsequent event has occurred.

Request management to inform the auditor of significant events arising after the accounts have been approved by the directors (and the audit report issued) but before the accounts have been approved by the shareholders.

Refer to APB Practice Notes, if revised financial statements are issued.

Consider changes in legislation, and enquiries, reviews or reports by regulatory bodies.

Review the outcome of areas of significant judgement, including accounting estimates, and litigation.

Perform an up-to-date review of material matters high-lighted during the course of the audit fieldwork.

Obtain written representations from management about post balance sheet events (SAS 440).

SAS 160

OTHER INFORMATION IN DOCUMENTS CONTAINING AUDITED FINANCIAL STATEMENTS

ISSUED MARCH 1995

Summary

Requires the auditor to consider the contents of other documents in the annual report of an entity before signing the audit report.

Key Points

Other information includes the directors' report (a legal requirement), the operating and financial review, the chairman's report, employment data, five year summaries, and ratios.

Auditors have a statutory responsibility to check that there are no inconsistencies between the financial statements and the directors' report. If there are, the audit report must refer to the inconsistencies.

Discuss any inconsistency between the financial statements and incorrectly presented data in "other information" with the directors. The objective should be to amend the "other information". If amended, no further action is required.

If not amended, consider:

- Whether the financial statements give a true and fair view (and the audit report implications if they do not) or

- Whether, if the financial statements do give a true and fair view, the auditor can continue with the audit engagement (consider resigning).

Application Notes

Near audit completion time, obtain and read the entire package that will contain the audited financial statements.

Request management to give the final package to the auditor for inspection before issue to the members of the entity.

Refer to any inconsistency between information in the directors' report and the financial statements in the audit report (statutory duty).

Consider whether there are any material inconsistencies (for example, do the statements in the operating and financial review really reflect the events of the year? Are graphs of selected information scaled fairly?). Discuss with management, directors or audit committee (as appropriate) with the objective of changing the "other information". Consider implications if corrective action is not taken. In extreme cases, consider withdrawal from the engagement.

SAS 200

PLANNING

ISSUED MARCH 1995

Summary

Gives guidance, in the context of recurring audits, on planning an audit.

Key Points

Plan to ensure that the audit is performed effectively, efficiently, and in a timely manner.

Document the overall audit plan for the assignment.

Matters to be documented include:

- Knowledge of the entity's business
- Risk and materiality
- Nature, timing and extent of procedures
- Co-ordination, direction, supervision and review
- Other matters (for example, terms of the engagement, nature and timing of reports, etc.).

Document an audit programme, which is both a set of instructions to those involved and a means of controlling the recording and correct completion of work.

Change the audit plan and programme during the audit if conditions change or there are unexpected test results.

Application Notes

Identify the critical audit areas and also the potential audit issues.

Perform analytical procedures.

Meet with management to discuss the engagement and to confirm preliminary results arising out of analytical procedures.

Discuss with management business issues, recent and future trend developments, changes in regulatory framework, etc. affecting the business.

If there is an internal audit team, consider how this will assist in the audit.

Consider the effect of related parties.

Decide whether the internal control systems are going to be relied on or whether more independent substantive evidence is required.

Consider using computer aided audit techniques (CAAT), if appropriate.

Examine the financial position of the entity.

Document the planning decisions and the intended scope and conduct of the audit in an overall audit plan.

Document an audit programme to achieve the objectives of the overall audit plan. Review the programme during the audit and, if unexpected results arise from audit procedures, revise the programme.

Set out a time plan for the audit, including:

- Stocktaking dates
- Audit start date
- Time to be spent in each audit area
- Contents of client's prepared schedules (and date expected)
- Review date(s)
- Client approval date.

If a group is involved, set out requirements for auditors of subsidiaries, including:

- Accounts completion dates
- Obtaining copies of reports to management, etc.

Assign staff appropriate to the risk levels and difficulties expected.

Consider the use of specialists on the audit engagement (for example, taxation experts, computer auditors, property valuers, etc.).

The audit partner should approve the audit plan and any revisions thereto.

SAS 210

KNOWLEDGE OF THE BUSINESS

ISSUED MARCH 1995

Summary

Sets out the standards required of an audit team in obtaining sufficient knowledge of the client's business to be able to undertake the audit effectively.

Key Points

In order to perform an audit of an entity to the highest standards, those involved must understand the business's operations, the industry(ies) involved and the markets for the products.

Accept an audit engagement only if one has sufficient knowledge to do a proper audit (either prior knowledge or easily obtainable subsequent knowledge).

At (or before) each following audit, update knowledge levels, identify major changes and re-assess audit procedures.

The audit partner must ensure audit staff have sufficient knowledge of the client's business and that any new information that becomes available to any audit staff is passed on to all the audit team.

Consider whether the financial statements are consistent with the audit team's knowledge of the business.

Knowledge requirements:

- General economic factors:
  - ◊ Interest rates
  - ◊ Finance availability
  - ◊ Inflation
  - ◊ Tariffs
  - ◊ Trade restrictions
- The industry:
  - ◊ Markets
  - ◊ Competition
  - ◊ Business risk
  - ◊ Adverse conditions
  - ◊ Key ratios/statistics
  - ◊ Accounting practices and problems
  - ◊ Environmental considerations
- The entity's management:
  - ◊ Structures — corporate, capital, and organisational
  - ◊ Management objectives, and philosophy
  - ◊ Board of directors
  - ◊ Internal audit experience
  - ◊ Incentive payments
  - ◊ Pressures
- The entity's business:
  - ◊ Products

◊ Markets

◊ Suppliers

◊ Expenses

◊ Research and development

◊ Inventories and locations

◊ Foreign exchange — assets, liabilities, transactions, hedging.

• Financial performance factors:

◊ Ratios

◊ Trends.

• Reporting environment:

◊ Law

◊ Statements of Auditing Standards

◊ Financial Reporting Standards

◊ Users' requirements.

Application Notes

Have a permanent audit file for all audit clients. In this file, keep information to enable any audit team member to readily meet the "knowledge requirements" of this SAS and to use for analytical procedure purposes (SAS 410). Keep the information as concise as possible. Maintain separate files for tax, audit, secretarial, correspondence. Make sure to update files each year (review at the end of the audit).

Meet clients regularly. At the audit planning stage, identify any significant changes in the business.

The audit partner should brief the audit team on developments in client's industry and business.

Suggested contents of a permanent audit file include:

- Summary of key financial ratios (historical record)
- List of main shareholdings
- List of directors, directors' shareholdings and options
- Brief notes on directors' experience, qualifications
- List of related parties
- Treasury policy and effect of exchange rates
- Sources of finance — summary of terms of loans and any special conditions or covenants
- Summary of critical accounting policies
- Summary of key risks and opportunities in the business
- Location of entity's premises, facilities, etc.
- Summary of key legislation and regulations affecting the entity
- Organisational chart(s) and job descriptions of key staff
- Summary of corporate objectives and management's policies and procedures to achieve same
- Summary of key products, services, market shares, etc.
- Copy of latest letter of engagement (SAS 140)
- Copy of last year's report to directors/management (SAS 610)

- Location of deeds of title to properties etc.

- Copies of latest valuations of properties, etc.

- Summary of any complex transactions undertaken by entity (for example, factoring, consignment stocks, securitisation, etc.)

- Summary of goodwill arising on each acquisition

- Summary of the information systems in use (SAS 310).

SAS 220

MATERIALITY AND THE AUDIT

ISSUED MARCH 1995

Summary

Gives guidance on the term "materiality", which affects both auditing and financial reporting.

Key Points

Materiality cannot be mathematically defined; it has both qualitative and quantitative aspects.

If the omission of a matter from (or an error in) the financial statements of an entity would influence a decision of one of the members, it is material.

Consider materiality when deciding on the design of audit procedures (preliminary assessment). Reconsider if test results indicate that the original assessment was incorrect.

Legal and regulatory requirements influence the materiality aspect of certain matters (for example, disclosure of directors' emoluments).

Consider materiality of total errors (specific errors found plus best estimate of projected errors) that have not been corrected in deciding whether the true and fair view is affected.

Application Notes

At audit planning stage, perform a preliminary assessment of materiality in relation to the financial statements.

Document the assessment of materiality and planned audit approach in audit plan. Ensure audit partner approval is obtained.

Keep a summary sheet in the audit file and note the effect of all errors found.

Consider the items on this summary sheet in the context of the overall effect on the results, balance sheet, and on particular items such as payroll costs, directors' remuneration, etc.

Estimate the effect of other possible errors not found and assess the implications (quantification is more reliable if statistical techniques are used).

During the audit, consider whether any errors detected require amendments in the nature, timing or extent of audit tests.

Consider the materiality impact of the previous period's unadjusted errors on the current year's results.

Obtain audit partner approval for the level of unadjusted misstatements. The auditor may have to request the directors to amend the entity's financial statements, if material.

SAS 230

WORKING PAPERS

ISSUED MARCH 1995

Summary

Sets out standards required for the content of working papers and the period for which these should be retained.

Key Points

Document all material matters of principle and judgement met during the audit to provide a record of the relevant facts on which the audit opinion was based.

Audit working papers should document:

- Planning and performance
- Supervision and review
- Evidence supporting the auditor's opinion.

Working papers are the property of the auditors and should be retained for at least six years (longer if they may be required).

Working papers should be kept confidential.

To provide audit evidence, working papers should record:

- What audit procedures were undertaken
- When they were undertaken
- By whom

- The reviewer's name and date.

Application Notes

Standardised working papers often help in ensuring the efficiency of the audit and in controlling the quality. Beware, however, of a stereotyped approach to audits.

Check that any schedules prepared by the client are correct.

Ensure that all working papers:

- State an objective
- Provide evidence of the work done, when and by whom
- Show what conclusion was reached
- Are approved by the reviewer (for example, manager/partner).

Keep working papers for a period of at least six years. Details of acquisitions of fixed assets, goodwill on the acquisition of an entity, etc. may need to be kept longer — consider putting these in the permanent audit file.

Before destruction of audit files, confirm that they are unlikely to be required in the future.

Maintain the following files (where appropriate) separately:

- Taxation
- Secretarial
- Audit (permanent and annual)

- Permanent financial statements

- Special engagements.

Update working papers to resolve any matters arising out of the review of the audit by the partner/manager.

Update permanent audit file where necessary (for example, new loan agreements or share/group structure changes).

Ensure safe custody of working papers during and after audit. Obtain audit partner approval for external access to files.

SAS 240

QUALITY CONTROL FOR AUDIT WORK

ISSUED MARCH 1995

Summary

Sets out the standards required in quality control both in the audit firm and the individual audit engagement.

Key Points

Establish quality control policies for the firm, to ensure that all audits are conducted in accordance with SASs.

Policies should include:

- Professional requirements
- Skills and competence required
- Not accepting (or retaining) clients that cannot be serviced properly
- Assignment of work and supervision requirements
- Consultation
- Monitoring of standards.

For each audit, the audit partner must apply the firm's policies taking into account the requirements of the specific audit.

The audit partner is responsible for ensuring that work carried out by the firm's staff can be relied upon in reaching the audit conclusion — the audit must be planned, supervised and reviewed.

The normal requirements are:

- Audit plan (background of business; possible auditing and accounting problems, and extent of testing required)

- Time budgets

- Competent staff for the job

- Supervision

- A review (to ensure tests are completed as planned, documented correctly and that conclusions are consistent with the test results).

Application Notes

Establish and document quality control policies and procedures to ensure all audit assignments are performed in accordance with SASs.

Communicate quality control policies and procedures to all staff.

Inform staff of changes in quality control policies and procedures.

Ensure the technical and professional competence of staff. Send staff on relevant courses to make them aware of updates in technical pronouncements.

Ensure that only staff with appropriate levels of skill, competence and experience are assigned to tasks.

Ensure that all work performed is adequately planned, directed, supervised, documented and reviewed.

Perform regular reviews of existing clients to confirm
the appropriateness of the firm continuing to serve as
auditor.

Evaluate prospective clients prior to accepting the engagement.

Monitor, on an independent basis, the effectiveness of
the operation of quality control policies and procedures.
Select a number of audits each year for review by another partner (if possible).

SAS 300

ACCOUNTING AND INTERNAL CONTROL SYSTEMS AND AUDIT RISK ASSESSMENT

ISSUED MARCH 1995

Summary

Sets out the standards required in assessing audit risk, developing audit programmes to reduce the risk to an acceptable level, and the necessity of understanding the accounting and internal control systems in use.

Key Points

There are three components in audit risk:

- **Inherent risk**: Risk of error or misstatement, assuming no internal controls

- **Control risk**: Risk of error or misstatement not prevented or detected by internal controls or accounting systems

- **Detection risk**: Risk that audit tests of transactions, balances, and analytical procedures will not detect a material error or misstatement.

Assess audit risk using professional judgement. Then design procedures to reduce to an acceptable (low) level of risk.

Understand the entity's accounting and internal control procedures — note that auditors are only concerned with controls relating to financial statement assertions (see SAS 400).

Inherent risk assessment is based on the experience of previous audits plus an evaluation of factors at financial statement, account balance and class of transactions levels.

Evaluate the effectiveness of the company's internal control systems in detecting and preventing errors or misstatements (preliminary assessment).

Plan tests of controls to reduce the levels of substantive tests. If the preliminary assessment is not supported by the results of the tests of the internal controls, modify the substantive tests accordingly.

Ensure that evidence is obtained that no changes have occurred in the internal control system, if relying on interim audit tests.

Perform some substantive procedures for all material account balances and transaction balances (analytical procedures may suffice in some cases).

The higher the risk, the greater the need to obtain more audit evidence.

If the risk cannot be reduced to acceptable levels, consider the audit report implications — perhaps even consider withdrawal from the audit.

In businesses where little segregation of duty is possible, it is likely that auditors will perform only substantive tests to obtain audit evidence and therefore will not need to evaluate or test internal control systems.

Application Notes

Assign audit staff with appropriate levels of skill, knowledge and experience to assess audit risk.

Document the accounting system (flowcharts are easier to understand — and update — than written compositions!).

Document the internal control system (the procedures being used by management to achieve the proper conduct of the business).

Assess the effectiveness of the system in identifying material errors in the financial statements. Plan the audit procedures accordingly.

To assess audit risk, examine the following areas:

- Items in the financial statements that are difficult to estimate (for example, contract work-in-progress valuation, or bad debts provision)

- Unusual transactions and journal entries (particularly near year end)

- Complex transactions, where the substance of the transactions are not easy to understand

- Assets that are easily misappropriated

- Involvement of related parties with the entity

- Extremely tight deadlines for reporting (soon after the year end) that increase the risk of error

- Profit-related bonuses for management

- Pressure to match budgets or profit forecasts

- Changes in key personnel during the period.

Design the planning approach to be taken (see SAS 200).

Perform substantive testing on all major items in the financial statements, even if the risk is assessed as low.

Increase the amount of substantive testing where internal controls are not assessed as effective — for many small clients, substantive tests only will be the norm.

Where reliance on controls is planned, confirm the effective operation of controls throughout the period by testing a sample of transactions. Consider whether there were any changes in the accounting or internal control systems during the financial period. Assess whether the results of tests confirm the initial risk assessment — if not, consider appropriate action.

Inform management of any weaknesses noted in either the accounting or internal control systems (see SAS 610).

SAS 400

AUDIT EVIDENCE

ISSUED MARCH 1995

Summary

Gives guidance on the procedures recommended to obtain audit evidence and establishes standards for the quantity and quality of evidence required.

Key Points

Obtain sufficient audit evidence to make reasonable conclusions in forming the audit opinion.

If appropriate evidence cannot be obtained, consider the implications for the audit report.

Check:

- The design of the internal control system

- That the system has operated effectively during the period (this applies if seeking audit evidence from testing the internal control systems).

The evidence from substantive tests undertaken should support the financial statement assertions.

Assertions are the explicit or implied representations by management embodied in financial statements. Normally audit evidence is required to support each financial statement assertions, which are:

- **Existence**: The asset or liability exists at a given date

- **Rights and obligations**: The asset or liability pertains to the entity

- **Occurrence**: A transaction or event pertaining to the entity has taken place during the period

- **Completeness**: No unrecorded assets, liabilities, transactions or events or no undisclosed items

- **Valuation**: Asset or liability is carried at an appropriate carrying value

- **Measurement**: A transaction or event is recorded at the proper amount and revenue or expense is allocated to the proper period

- **Presentation and disclosure**: An item is disclosed, classified and described in accordance with applicable legislation and accounting standards.

Audit evidence is obtained by one or more of the following procedures:

- Inspection

- Observation

- Enquiry and confirmation

- Computation

- Analytical procedures.

Substantive tests are of two types:

- Tests of details of transactions and balances

- Analytical procedures.

Application Notes

Test (and document) all major balance sheet and profit and loss figures by inspection, observation, enquiry, confirmation, and computation.

For less material items and transactions, use analytical procedures.

Report to management any weaknesses noted in tests of the accounting and/or internal control systems.

Obtain external evidence (for example, confirmation from the entity's solicitor) about the existence of litigation, acquisition or disposal of assets rather than internal evidence.

Obtain, where possible, confirmations of major items (for example, debtors and bank confirmations) directly to the auditor's offices.

List material oral representations, for which no documentary evidence is available, so that these can be included in management's letter of representation.

Consider the implications for the audit report of insufficient evidence.

Revise the audit programme, where appropriate, in the light of results of tests of the accounting and internal control systems, analytical review procedures and substantive tests.

Obtain audit evidence up to the date of the audit report (SAS 150).

Consider contingencies and possible illegal acts.

Confirm compliance with laws and regulations (SAS 120).

Consider the use of computer aided audit techniques (CAAT).

Investigate audit differences and prepare a summary of unadjusted differences.

SAS 410

ANALYTICAL PROCEDURES

ISSUED MARCH 1995

Summary

Gives guidance and establishes standards as to when analytical procedures should be used during an audit.

Key Points

Analytical procedures should be applied both at the planning stage (to identify areas of potential risk) and the overall review stage (to ensure the financial statements are consistent with the conclusions arrived at) of an audit.

Analytical procedures involve the analysis of significant ratios and trends in the business and the investigation of fluctuations or deviations from expected patterns.

Analytical procedures can be used on their own as a substantive procedure for audit evidence — normally for items that are not material.

Investigate significant fluctuations or deviations from expected patterns — obtain explanations and other supporting evidence.

If no explanations are available (or are inadequate), decide on extra audit procedures to be undertaken to ascertain the reason for the fluctuation or deviation.

Application Notes

For each client, build up a "Key ratios/figures" profile and keep this on the permanent audit file.

The profile could include, for instance:

- Turnover (by product, geographical area, major customers)

- Gross profit (by product, geographical area)

- Sales commission

- Bad debts

- Payroll costs

- Major costs of production

- Employee numbers

- Net assets

- Stock turnover

- Market share.

Analyse the key ratios of the entity at the planning stage of the audit. Compare to previous years and against budget. Compare with similar entities, if information is available.

Consider the use of the computer as a tool to assist in developing analytical procedures.

Use non-financial information where available (for example, production quantities adjusted for stock movements to verify total sales volume) in addition to financial data.

Discuss with management the reasons for any unusual deviations from previous years or from expected results. Assess the implications of the discussions for planning audit procedures.

Consider whether the data analysed is relevant and reliable — test controls over the preparation of data.

At or near the end of the audit, perform appropriate analytical procedures to confirm that the original analysis was valid and that the financial statements are consistent with the auditor's knowledge and understanding of the business.

SAS 420
AUDIT OF ACCOUNTING ESTIMATES

ISSUED MARCH 1995

Summary

Gives guidance on, and sets standards for, the audit of accounting estimates made by management, that are included in financial statements.

Key Points

Auditors are likely to exercise more judgement when examining accounting estimates as evidence supporting same is generally more persuasive than conclusive.

Accounting estimates normally include amounts relating to:

- Net realisable value and obsolescence of stock
- Depreciation
- Deferred taxation
- Outcome of legal cases pending
- Construction work-in-progress
- Provisions for warranties
- Amortisation period of development costs.

To audit an accounting estimate, the auditor should do at least one of the following:

- Examine how management arrived at the estimate
- Obtain an independent estimate

- Review subsequent events that support the estimate made.

Assess the reasonableness of each estimate in the light of other evidence obtained during the audit and the auditor's knowledge of the business (and ensure adequate disclosure, if appropriate).

Towards the end of the audit, assess the reasonableness of all accounting estimates for the period in aggregate to ensure that the sum of the reasonable differences are not biased in one direction.

Application Notes

At the audit planning stage, assess the risks in accounting estimates that may result in a material misstatement in the financial statements.

Discuss with management the policies and procedures in place for the timely identification and correct accounting for accounting estimates. Report any weaknesses noted and suggest improvements.

Consider skills, competence and experience of entity staff responsible for preparing the accounting estimates.

Compare prior period accounting estimates with actual results for accuracy. Check that differences are properly accounted for.

Consider the assumptions underlying the calculation of the accounting estimates.

Test the calculations of the accounting estimates.

Consider the accuracy and completeness of the data used in the calculation of accounting estimates.

Consider management approval for the accounting estimates (include in the letter of representation).

Perform an appropriate subsequent events review to assess the accuracy of the accounting estimates (see SAS 150).

Consider the use of independent expertise, where appropriate.

Tests for usual accounting estimates may include:

- **Stock obsolescence**: Obtain aged listing of stock (physical inspection can sometimes suffice). Compare this with normal stock turnover for each product

- **Net realisable values**: Check post year-end sales values for major products

- **Depreciation**: Compare to previous year; check calculations on new additions; check sample of items fully depreciated (ask whether any of these still in use)

- **Warranties**: Examine sales documentation to see whether warranties have been given; compare actual result for the year against the previous estimate; consider the appropriateness of the accounting policy, if long-term warranties are given

- **Deferred taxation**: Obtain capital expenditure plans and check directors' meetings for evidence of approval; consider the effect if projects are delayed

- **Legal cases**: Obtain a letter from the entity's solicitor setting out details of any legal cases pending, together with likely outcomes

- **Construction work-in-progress**: Obtain assessments from the entity's architects as to likely final outcome of each project and any known potential risks.

SAS 430

AUDIT SAMPLING

ISSUED MARCH 1995

Summary

Sets out the standards required when using sampling techniques to select items that can be evaluated for audit evidence and applying the conclusions reached to the whole population from which the items have been selected.

Key Points

Audit sampling involves selecting less than 100 per cent of items within an account balance or class of transactions, performing tests and using the results to form a conclusion regarding the rest of the items.

If statistical sampling is used, mathematically constructed conclusions can be reached from the results whereas if non-statistical sampling is used the auditor's opinion is based on judgement alone.

Consider the sampling risk, allowable error and expected error when deciding on the sample size.

Compare the conclusion that would be reached if the entire population was tested as against the conclusion reached from testing the sample — this is the "sampling risk".

The allowable error is the maximum auditors will accept without changing their opinion — if the allowable error is to be small, a large sample is needed.

If errors are expected, select a sufficiently large sample to ensure that the actual error is less than the expected error.

In sampling, ensure that all items in the population being tested have an opportunity of being picked.

Sampling methods in normal use are:

• Random (using random number tables)

• Systematic (constant interval after a random start)

• Haphazard (may be difficult to ensure an unbiased sample).

Analyse the errors found — consider their nature, cause and possible effect on other aspects of the audit.

Project the errors found to the population tested — reassess the sampling risk. If risk has increased too much, perform other audit procedures (the result may be an adjustment to the financial statements).

Application Notes

At the audit planning stage, consider the use of sampling techniques as an audit tool. This is most likely to be effective where:

• There is a large number of insignificant items

• The population consists mainly of routine transactions

- It has been decided to adopt a substantive audit approach.

At the outset, specify the audit objectives to be achieved through sampling.

Confirm that the population sample is appropriate to achieve the specified audit objective.

Consider different sampling techniques, selecting one that ensures the sample is representative of the population.

Avoid haphazard selection of samples (where possible).

Use systematic or random number tables, which assume all items in the population have equal chance of selection.

Stratify the population where appropriate — for example, confirm all debtor balances over £x and a small sample of those under £x.

Define the conditions that constitute an error.

If some errors are expected, make the sample size big enough so that the errors found will be representative of the population.

Evaluate sample results — consider the level of errors found and project this across the entire population using a basis of projection consistent with the basis of the sample selection.

Take the probable overall error to the error summary sheet (see SAS 220) — not just the errors found.

Extend the tests if a common cause of errors is seen —
concentrate on just the problem area.

Re-assess the sampling risk if the projected error ex-
ceeds the allowable error. If the risk is unacceptable,
consider extending the audit procedures or performing
alternative audit procedures.

SAS 440

MANAGEMENT REPRESENTATIONS

ISSUED MARCH 1995

Summary

Sets standards for evaluation, documentation and use of important representations made by management during an audit.

Key Points

The directors are responsible for the financial statements — the auditor should obtain evidence that the directors acknowledge this responsibility.

Acceptable audit evidence includes minutes of board meetings, a written letter or a signed copy of the financial statements incorporating a statement of directors' responsibility.

Representations from management on material matters in financial statements are often necessary for audit evidence — obtain these in writing.

Management representations are not a substitute for other audit evidence where this is available.

Investigate the reason if audit evidence casts doubt on management representations (Which is incorrect? Was there a misunderstanding? What is the effect on the audit?).

Where written representations on an important matter are not given by management, this constitutes a limitation of scope in audit. Can the auditor rely on other representations? Consider the effect on the audit report.

Application Notes

Instead of a separate letter, the signatures of the directors on the directors' report and on the statement of directors' responsibilities will be sufficient evidence of the directors' approval of the accounts and their acknowledgement of responsibilities.

Set out the responsibilities of the directors in the letter of engagement.

During the audit, list all material representations received where no other audit evidence was available, and include these in the letter of representation.

In a group situation, obtain letters of representation regarding both the group accounts and the parent company.

Investigate the reasons for any discrepancy between representations made by management and other evidence obtained during the audit.

If management will not sign the letter of representation, consider the implications for the audit report (limitation of scope). Consider why the directors will not sign.

The date of the letter of representation should be the same day as the audit report approval, if feasible (or as near to that date as is possible).

Items that may need to be included in management's letter of representation:

- Details of guarantees, etc. issued by the entity
- Basis of research and development costs deferred
- Stocks — valuation/risk of obsolescence
- Contract work-in-progress — directors not aware of any unforeseen costs
- Basis of deferred taxation
- Details of "related parties" of the entity
- Directors' view of the outcome of legal cases pending
- Doubtful debts provision
- Capital expenditure commitments
- Valuation of unquoted investments
- Compliance with laws and regulations
- All material oral representations made during the audit.

Note: The letter of representation should include only items where the matters of fact are confined solely to management or areas that involve significant levels of directors' estimates/judgement.

SAS 450

OPENING BALANCES AND COMPARATIVES

ISSUED MARCH 1995

Summary

Sets out, in the context of both recurring audits and first year engagements, the necessity to ensure the opening balance sheet figures and comparatives are correctly stated.

Key Points

Compare the opening balances in nominal ledger to the closing balance of the preceding period — these must agree, unless there have been prior year adjustments or accounting policy changes.

Make sure there are no material errors in opening balances — if comparatives are adjusted for material errors, disclosure must be made.

Account for, and disclose, any changes in accounting policies.

If previous years' statements were qualified and the matter is:

- **Still unresolved**: Qualify with regard to opening balances and comparatives

- **Still unresolved but does not affect opening balances**: Qualify with regard to comparatives

- **Resolved**: Give an explanation of how treated.

Incoming auditors assume audit responsibility for comparatives — review last year's accounts, compare them with the current period and the comparatives.

If the comparatives have not been audited, disclose this clearly.

Consultations with previous auditors are normally held only to obtain clarification of significant accounting matters.

If the accounts have been qualified by previous auditors, pay special attention to the area qualified.

Application Notes

Agree the opening trial balance to last year's balance sheet.

Review the journal entries made at the start of the financial year.

Check that the accounting policies have not altered — if altered, ensure the comparatives are changed to reflect each new policy and that proper disclosure is made in the financial statements.

Consider the appropriateness of any change in the accounting policies.

Check that any matters qualified in last year's audit report are properly treated (see Key Points above).

Review the current year's financial statements to ensure that the previous years' audited figures are correctly disclosed. Disclose any restatement/regrouping of comparative figures.

Ensure adequate disclosure in the financial statements if the comparatives are unaudited. Consider implications for audit report.

Consider, in the current year, whether the previous year's figures are free from material misstatement (for example, review the outcome of material prior year accounting estimates — see SAS 420).

Ensure the correct and adequate disclosure of any amendment to comparatives required due to subsequent material error being discovered/noted.

SAS 460

RELATED PARTIES

ISSUED NOVEMBER 1995

Summary

Provides guidance on the audit of related party transactions and their disclosure in financial statements in accordance with Financial Reporting Standard 8, *Related Party Dislosure.*

Key Points

Directors are obliged to disclose:

- Material transactions with related parties

- The controlling party and, if different, the ultimate controlling party (even if no transactions have taken place).

A related party can be an individual, group of individuals, a partnership or other business entity where there is an ability to influence (or be influenced) directly or indirectly the operations of the reporting entity. (Family members of key management of the entity and its parent are also assumed to be related parties.)

Auditors should design audit procedures to ensure all material related party transactions are identified and adequately disclosed in the financial statements.

Assess the risk of unidentified material related party transactions.

Consider the materiality of transactions in relation to both the reporting entity and the other party.

Note: Smaller entities reporting in accordance with the Financial Reporting Standard for Smaller Entities should consider materiality only in relation to the reporting entity.

Obtain written representations from the directors confirming full disclosure of related party transactions and, where applicable, the controlling party (and ultimate controlling party).

Consider the implications for the audit report if disclosure is inadequate or sufficient audit evidence is not available.

Application Notes

At the audit planning stage, obtain a list of related parties (in writing) from management. Keep this in the permanent audit file and update each year.

Design procedures to check the recording of transactions with related parties (is such recording part of the normal accounting system or a special "once-off" analysis?).

Check/review the related party disclosures of transactions for the current reporting period. Obtain appropriate audit evidence.

Consider whether there are other transactions not reported. Be aware of transactions with extended terms of credit, unusual terms of trade, etc.

Ensure that the audit staff inform the audit partner if they become aware of any material related party transaction(s) not among the transactions listed by the directors.

Ensure that auditors of foreign components of the entity are aware of the requirements of this SAS. Provide details of known related party transactions to the auditors concerned.

Ensure that appropriate reference to related party transactions and disclosures are included in the letter of representation.

SAS 470

OVERALL REVIEW OF FINANCIAL STATEMENTS

ISSUED MARCH 1995

Summary

Sets out the standards required to be met by auditors in making a final review of the financial statements before signing the audit report.

Key Points

At the end of an audit, auditors must review the financial statements, and the audit evidence obtained, to ensure there is a reasonable basis for their audit opinion.

Ensure the financial statements comply with accounting standards and company law requirements.

Ensure the financial statements are consistent with other information and with the results of the audit opinion reached on the basis of audit testing.

Application Notes

Assign the task of overall review of the financial statements to a person with an appropriate level of knowledge and experience.

Allow sufficient time for review before the sign-off deadline.

Use a company accounts checklist each year — retain it on the audit file, duly signed off by the appropriate staff and audit partner. Ensure that the checklist contains the latest Financial Reporting Standards requirements.

Use a checklist to ensure support for financial statements is complete — retain it on file. The checklist will normally include the following:

- Support/evidence of profit and loss account and balance sheet items (including analytical review)

- Company accounts checklist (as previously mentioned)

- Subsequent events review

- Commitments and contingencies review

- Solicitors' letters and experts' reports

- Extracts from minutes — shareholders, directors, audit committee or management meetings

- Lease commitments

- Complex transactions — substance over form review

- Insurance review

- Reports to management/directors/audit committee — and response

- Consideration of laws and regulations applying to entity

- Review of directors' report and other information

- Directors' emoluments, loans, options

- Pension scheme review

- Related parties information/disclosure

- Going concern period evaluation.

Review the accounts package (including "other informa-tion" being sent to shareholders) to ensure there is ade-quate disclosure of material items.

Confirm that the accounting policies are appropriate and are consistently applied.

Agree any amendments to the financial statements with management, the directors, or the audit committee (as appropriate).

Consider whether items included in management's let-ter of representation are adequately disclosed, where necessary, in the financial statements.

Consider whether the analytical procedures (SAS 410) disclose any information that may affect the presenta-tion or disclosure of items in the financial statements.

SAS 500

CONSIDERING THE WORK OF INTERNAL AUDIT

ISSUED MARCH 1995

Summary

Sets out the standards required when considering using work done by a client's internal audit function to assist in planning the audit.

Key Points

External auditors have sole responsibility for the audit opinion expressed on a set of financial statements.

Work carried out by internal auditors may be useful to external auditors but the auditor must realise that the objectives of internal audit are determined by management and are different from the external auditors' objectives.

Assess the effectiveness of internal audit work where relevant to external audit.

Criteria:

• Status of internal audit within entity (any constraints placed on internal audit activity?)

• Scope of function — management action on recommendations

• Technical competence of audit team

- Internal control planning, supervision, review and documentation.

Evaluate any specific internal audit work (this may involve testing to ensure it is adequate) used to reduce extent of external audit work.

If not adequate, revise tests planned to obtain sufficient evidence to support audit conclusion.

Application Notes

At the planning stage, make a preliminary assessment of whether the use of the internal audit function can assist in the audit, by reducing the amount of testing required.

Agree with management, the directors or audit committee (as appropriate) the use of the internal audit function for the purpose of the external audit.

Meet with the internal audit manager and assess the internal audit function.

Examine the scope of the internal audit team, their experience, the documentation and reports issued.

Obtain copies of internal audit reports — review actions taken by management subsequent to the reports.

Agree in advance with the internal auditors the tests, documentation and sampling methods to be undertaken and the timing thereof.

Supervise internal audit staff and review their work, where relied upon.

If, after review, the internal audit work is deemed to be inadequate, decide what extra tests or evidence are required to meet the audit objectives.

Liaise with the internal audit function at regular intervals during the year.

Consider using the internal audit function to assess procedures not directly impacting on the financial statements (for example, compliance with, and monitoring of, laws and regulations affecting the entity).

SAS 510

THE RELATIONSHIP BETWEEN PRINCIPAL AUDITORS AND OTHER AUDITORS

ISSUED MARCH 1995

Summary

Sets out the standards applicable where one or more components included in the financial statements of an entity are audited by other auditors.

Key Points

Principal auditors must ensure that the work carried out by other auditors provides sufficient audit evidence.

Auditors should only accept the position of principal auditor if satisfied that their participation is sufficient to give a proper audit opinion.

Check that the other auditors are professionally qualified to undertake the audit of the component(s).

Check that the other auditors' procedures are adequate — (for example, questionnaires/checklists, review of working papers).

Discuss significant findings of other auditors both with the other auditors and with the management of the component.

Other auditors are responsible for the audit opinion on the component they are auditing. They should co-operate with, and assist the principal auditor (they may have to obtain permission from the component's management to communicate with the principal auditor — if this is refused, they must notify the principal auditor).

Principal auditors have sole responsibility for their audit opinion.

Do not refer to other auditors in the audit opinion. However, if a component's audit report is qualified, it may be necessary for the principal auditor to reflect that fact in their audit report.

The Companies Act (s.389A, UK; s.397, Northern Ireland; s.196, Republic of Ireland) imposes a duty on a subsidiary and its auditors to give information and explanations reasonably required to the principal auditor to enable them to carry out their duties as the auditor of the holding company.

Application Notes

Consider, as principal auditor:

- The materiality of the components audited by other auditors

- The competency of the other auditors, the adequacy of their knowledge of the business and their independence — obtain written confirmation at an early stage.

Decide whether it is appropriate to act as principal auditor.

If acting as principal auditor, ensure the letter of engagement makes clear to the directors of the entity their responsibilities regarding the group financial statements.

Set out in the letter of engagement what information the auditors of components should notify (and when) to the principal auditor.

Agree at the planning stage, for each component:

- The material areas that need special attention
- Reporting requirements for inter-group transactions and related party transactions
- Timetable for audit completion
- Contact names.

Review other auditors' working papers — the more material the component, the more regular the review.

Obtain and review a written summary of the other auditors' procedures and findings. Confirm compliance with requirements set out in the planning correspondence.

Assess the impact of the other auditors' findings on the group audit.

Arrange for the other auditors to submit copies of the managements' letters of representation (SAS 440) and their reports to management (SAS 610) with the financial statements of the components they audit.

Update the permanent audit file — knowledge of the business section — with any relevant information.

Make special arrangements to obtain the co-operation of auditors of components of the entity that are not subsidiaries — for example, joint ventures, associated companies, quasi-subsidiaries.

7

8 *Auditing Standards*

SAS 520

USING THE WORK OF AN EXPERT

ISSUED MARCH 1995

Summary

Sets out the standards required if using the work of an expert to obtain audit evidence.

Key Points

Auditors are not expected to have the expertise of a person qualified in another profession or occupation (for example, an actuary or engineer).

Ensure that the independence, objectivity and integrity of the auditors is not affected if the "expert" engaged for an assignment is employed by them or is associated with them.

To determine whether the use of an expert is needed, consider:

• Whether the matter is material

• The risk of error or misstatement in financial statements

• The quantity and quality of other audit evidence.

If auditors need to use experts, discuss with management — if management is unable or unwilling, look for other audit evidence that may be available.

Ensure that the expert chosen is professionally competent and objective.

Review the expert's terms of reference to ensure that the scope of work is adequate to provide appropriate audit evidence.

Review the expert's findings and ensure that (if the auditor is happy) these are properly disclosed in financial statements or that they support the financial statement assertions.

If there is inconsistency between other audit evidence and the results of the expert's work, attempt to resolve the inconsistency by discussing it with the entity's management and the expert.

Application Notes

At the planning stage determine which, if any, of the financial statement assertions require to be evidenced by specialists ("experts") such as actuaries, architects, lawyers, valuers, surveyors, engineers, etc.

Agree with management the most appropriate expert, who must preferably be independent of the entity. If management is not willing, consider whether this constitutes a limitation of audit scope.

Confirm the integrity, objectivity, and professional competence of the expert.

Set out, with management, the terms of reference for the expert:

- What evidence is needed
- The purpose of the report
- Whether the report (or extracts) will be published or referred to

- Assumptions, bases to be used (ensure consistency with previous reports).

- Timing of the work.

If management has already engaged the expert, request a meeting to explain the audit objective to the expert and obtain confirmation that the expert's report is useful for audit purposes.

Confirm that the expert has had adequate access to all data and information necessary for the purpose of the report.

Obtain and review the expert's report and consider the implications for the audit — consider whether the results are consistent with other audit evidence.

Do not refer to the work of the expert in the audit report if accepting the work as valid audit evidence. Consider whether appropriate disclosure of the expert's work is required in the financial statements.

SAS 600

AUDITORS' REPORTS ON FINANCIAL STATEMENTS

ISSUED MAY 1993

Summary

Establishes standards and gives guidance on the form and content of audit reports issued on financial statements.

Key Points

The audit report is the final product of the audit of the financial statements of an entity. In completing the audit, ensure that all the following aspects have been considered (and documented!):

- Responsibility

- Planning, controlling and recording

- Accounting systems and internal control

- Evidence

- Using the work of others.

The audit report must give a clear expression of opinion, based on an assessment of the evidence obtained.

The report must:

- Identify those to whom it is addressed — for example, the shareholders of ABC Limited

- Identify which statements are being reported on — for example, *the historical cost statements (as modi-*

fied by the revaluation of certain fixed assets) for the year ended (date)

- Set out the responsibilities of the directors — unless these are adequately covered in another part of the financial statements or accompanying information

- Set out the responsibilities of the auditor, including an explanation of what constitutes an audit — testing, assessing estimates, checking accounting policies, and disclosure and presentation of information. Also the fact that the audit was planned so as to obtain all information and sufficient evidence to ensure the financial statements are free from material misstatement

- Explain the basis of the audit opinion

- Give the audit opinion — only refer to the profit and loss account and balance sheet (there is no requirement to report on other statements)

- Contain the signature (written or typed) of the auditor

- Be dated.

Fundamental Uncertainty
If a fundamental uncertainty is adequately accounted for and properly disclosed, include an explanatory paragraph but no qualification.

Limitation of Audit Scope
Where the auditor is unable to get enough evidence to reach an unqualified opinion:

- He or she must describe the limitation

- If its effect is material, issue a disclaimer of opinion

- If its effect is not material, qualify and explain possible adjustments.

Disagreement on Accounting Treatment or Disclosure
Describe, give implications and quantify (where possible) the effect and:

- If the financial accounts are misleading, give an adverse opinion

- For other material items, qualify using an "except for" paragraph.

Signing and Dating of Audit Report
To be done only after the financial statements, directors' report, etc. have been approved by the directors and the package reviewed by the auditor. (Normally only a short interval should elapse between board approval and audit signature; if a long period elapses, the auditor must ensure the accounts are still approved.)

Example of an Unqualified Audit Report — UK Company

AUDITORS' REPORT TO THE SHAREHOLDERS
OF ABC LIMITED

We have audited the financial statements on pages 5 to 18 which have been prepared under the historical cost convention (as modified by the revaluation of certain fixed assets) and the accounting policies set out on page 5.

Respective Responsibilities of Directors and Auditors:
As described on page 3 the company's directors are responsible for the preparation of financial statements. It is our responsibility to form an independent

opinion, based on our audit, on those statements and to report our opinion to you.

Basis of Opinion:
We conducted our audit in accordance with Auditing Standards issued by the Auditing Practices Board. An audit includes examination, on a test basis, of evidence relevant to the amounts and disclosures in the financial statements. It also includes an assessment of the significant estimates and judgements made by the directors in the preparation of the financial statements, and of whether the accounting policies are appropriate to the company's circumstances, consistently applied and adequately disclosed.

We planned and performed our audit so as to obtain all the information and explanations which we considered necessary in order to provide us with sufficient evidence to give reasonable assurance that the financial statements are free from material misstatement, whether caused by fraud or other irregularity or error. In forming our opinion we also evaluated the overall adequacy of the presentation of information in the financial statements.

Opinion:
In our opinion the financial statements give a true and fair view of the state of the company's affairs as at 31 December 1997 and of its profit for the year then ended and have been properly prepared in accordance with the Companies Act 1985.

U No Who & Co.
Registered Auditors
Blank Street.
1 March 1998

In the Republic of Ireland, the opinion section would read:

> In our opinion the financial statements give a true and fair view of the state of the company's affairs as at 31 December 1997 and of its profit for the year then ended and have been properly prepared in accordance with the Companies Acts 1963 to 1990.

> We have obtained all the information and explanations we consider necessary for the purposes of our audit. In our opinion, proper books of account have been kept by the company. The financial statements are in agreement with the books of account.

> In our opinion, the information given in the directors' report on page 2 is consistent with the financial statements.

> The net assets of the company, as stated in the balance sheet on page 7, are more than half of the amount of its called up share capital and, in our opinion, on that basis there did not exist at 31 December 1997 a financial situation which, under section 40(1) of the Companies (Amendment) Act 1983, would require the convening of an extraordinary general meeting of the company.

Statement of directors' responsibilities — example for a large UK company

If this is not presented separately in the financial statements, it must be included in the second paragraph of the audit opinion:

> Company law requires the directors to prepare financial statements for each financial year that give a

true and fair view of the state of affairs of the company and of the profit or loss of the company for that period. In preparing those financial statements, the directors are required to:

- Select suitable accounting policies and then apply them consistently

- Make judgements and estimates that are reasonable and prudent

- State whether applicable accounting standards have been followed, subject to any material departures disclosed and explained in the financial statements (large companies only)

- Prepare the financial statements on the going concern basis unless it is inappropriate to presume that the company will continue in business.

The directors are responsible for keeping proper accounting records that disclose with reasonable accuracy at any time the financial position of the company and to enable them to ensure that the financial statements comply with the Companies Act 1985. They are also responsible for safeguarding the assets of the company and hence for taking reasonable steps for the prevention and detection of fraud and other irregularities.

Application Notes

The audit partner must review the audit file and ensure that the support for the financial statements checklist (see SAS 470) is complete.

Summarise the important points of the financial statements and the entity's business.

Review the summary of unadjusted audit differences.

Consider the appropriateness of the going concern "foreseeable future" period chosen as regards additional disclosure (if less than one year) and whether a longer period is necessary.

Check that a letter of representation and a statement of directors' responsibilities are obtained.

Discuss with management, the directors, and audit committee (as appropriate) the basis of the audit opinion (see Key Points above). Confirm that no unusual matters have occurred or arisen since the audit work was completed.

Agree with management, the directors, and audit committee (as appropriate) whether extra audit evidence can be obtained to overcome the limitation (if any) of audit scope.

Inform management, the directors, and audit committee (as appropriate) of any changes required in accounting treatment or disclosure in the financial statements to avoid qualification or a disclaimer of opinion.

Explain the reasons for the wording of the audit report and notes in the financial statements if there is a 'fundamental uncertainty' consideration.

Obtain the directors' (minuted) approval of, and signatures to, the financial statements package.

Issue the audit report, date it and sign as Registered Auditor.

Note: Refer to Bulletin 1997/3 (see page 189) regarding the implications of the FRSSE from the auditors' report on the financial statements of small enterprises

SAS 610

REPORTS TO DIRECTORS OR MANAGEMENT

ISSUED MARCH 1995

Summary

Sets out the requirements regarding the reporting of weaknesses, in both accounting and other internal control systems, to directors and management.

Key Points

A report is an important result of an audit.

Report material weaknesses identified in the accounting and internal control systems and suggest improvements.

Suggest improvements in efficiency identified during the audit.

Comment on errors (whether adjusted or not) and particular accounting policies and practices that appear to be inappropriate.

A letter or report to management cannot excuse a qualification where this is required by SAS 600.

Normally address the letter or report to management, to the board of directors or the audit committee. Request a reply showing actions, if any, to be taken by directors.

Make the report immediately after completion of audit.

Consider the audit implications of matters raised in previous reports.

Make sure permission is received from management of subsidiaries before informing the parent entity's management of contents of management reports relating to the relevant subsidiary.

To reduce liability to a third party, state in the report that:

- It was prepared for entity's use

- Permission is required before it may be disclosed to anyone else

- No responsibility is accepted towards any person other than the addressee(s) of the report.

Application Notes

During the audit, note all matters that should be brought to the attention of management, the directors or audit committee (as appropriate).

Address the report to the level appropriate in the entity — that is, those who can act on the points raised.

Report (and suggest improvements) on failures and weaknesses identified in the accounting and internal control systems.

Comment on the appropriateness of the accounting policies followed.

Comment on the implications of foreseeable accounting or legislative changes.

Matters raised should include references to description of observations, suggested improvements and the benefit of action by the management.

Suggest improvements in other (non-financial) areas identified during the audit.

Reports should be constructive and timely. Consider reporting after the interim audit and again after the year-end audit.

Follow up matters raised in previous reports and include them in the current year's report, where appropriate.

Request a response from management.

The report should explicitly state:

- That it is not comprehensive and excludes items that may arise from a special review
- That the report is for the entity and should not be distributed to third parties without prior consent.

Do not issue a copy of the report other than to the entity (unless permission is given).

SAS 620

THE AUDITORS' RIGHT AND DUTY TO REPORT TO REGULATORS IN THE FINANCIAL SECTOR

ISSUED MARCH 1994

Summary

Sets out standards to be met by auditors of businesses in the financial sector to fulfil their statutory duty to report to regulators in certain circumstances.

Key Points

Legal requirements to report to regulators are set out in:

UK

- Building Societies Act 1986

- Banking Act 1987

- Financial Services Act 1986

- Insurance Companies Act 1982

- Friendly Societies Act 1992

Note: Statutory Instruments set out the duty to report under the above Acts. Charities and Pensions were added in 1995.

Ireland

- Building Societies Act 1989

- Central Bank Act 1989

- Trustees Savings Bank Act 1989

- Insurance Act 1989

- European Communities (UCITS) Regulations 1989

- Unit Trust Act 1990

- ACC Bank Act 1992

- ICC Bank Act 1992

- Companies Act 1990 (section 258).

In addition to reporting on financial statements, auditors have extra reporting responsibilities to regulators under the above Acts.

Where the auditor becomes aware, during the course of the audit, of certain information, a report is required by the regulator on matters specified by law or regulation (statutory responsibility).

Matters of significance to a regulator include:

- Possible breach of an entity's authorisation

- Failure to meet statutory or regulatory requirements

- Going concern doubts

- A qualified audit report.

Notify the appropriate regulator as soon as possible where there is a responsibility to report and if the matter is likely to be of significance to the regulator.

Normally agree the report with the directors but note that statutory responsibility takes precedence over the auditor's duty to the entity.

If the matter casts doubt on the integrity of the directors, the auditor should report directly to the regulator
(without informing the directors). The duty to report
does not mean that the auditor must carry out specific
work; report only if the matter arises as part of normal
audit procedures.

The contents of a report might include:

- The name of the entity
- The statutory power under which the report is made
- The fact that the report is made in accordance with
  SAS 620
- Context
- Subject matter
- Auditor's signature and date of report
- A request for confirmation of receipt.

Planning, supervision and control of audits of regulated
bodies should be performed in a manner similar to other
audits (the knowledge level of the special rules etc. applying must be high — for example, the scope of the entity's authorisation).

Where there are matters arising, not covered by rules of
reporting, but which are important, initially request the
directors to notify the regulator; if this is not done, the
auditor should notify the regulator.

When drafting the audit opinion on the financial statements, consider the effect of matters notified to the
regulator.

The statutory responsibility to report information to regulators relates to information obtained in the course of the audit. Information or knowledge obtained in other capacities may not normally be disclosed, as it would breach the duty of confidence.

Since 1996, auditors of an entity closely linked to a regulated entity of which they are also auditors have a duty to report information obtained (while auditing the closely-linked entity) about the regulated entity.

Application Notes

Maintain, on the permanent audit file, a copy of relevant legislation applicable to the client.

Maintain, on the permanent audit file, a copy of the relevant APB Practice Note (relating to banks, building societies, investment businesses, insurance companies and friendly societies, charities and pension schemes, as appropriate).

Ensure all audit staff are aware of the contents of legislation and Practice Note(s) applicable to each client.

Ensure all audit staff immediately notify the audit partner of any breach in regulations noted. Consider whether the breach is of material significance to the regulator (duty to report direct without delay) or not significant (right to report direct).

Note: Material significance to the regulator may not be material in relation to the financial statements.

Design procedures within the firm to ensure that the audit partner is informed of any non-audit work undertaken for a regulated client and that they consider the results of this non-audit work when planning (and reviewing) the audit.

AUDITING STANDARDS AND THE SMALLER COMPANY

Auditing standards are intended to be applied to all audits of financial statements (unless there is a specific exemption in a standard).

Audit Exemptions

In Ireland, the Company Law Reform Commission recommended that companies with a turnover under £100,000 should be exempt from the audit requirement. In March 1995, a commitment to implement this recommendation was given by the government, though no legislation has been enacted to date.

From 1994, companies in the UK that met the criteria below were exempt from the audit requirement:

- Balance sheet total less than £1,400,000
- Turnover less than £90,000.

The turnover limit was increased in 1997 to £350,000 for companies other than charities.

Exemption from audit can only be blocked if shareholder(s) holding 10 per cent or more of the shares of the company deposit a notice in writing at the company's registered office at least one month prior to the financial year end requesting an audit.

Charitable companies whose balance sheet total is less than £1,400,000 but whose turnover is between £90,000 and £250,000 can opt for an accountant's report.

The audit exemption option is not available to PLCs, banks, or insurance companies, regardless of their qualification on balance sheet or turnover grounds.

Group companies can avail of the audit exemption if the group satisfies the conditions for a small group.

Directors of companies that avail of the audit exemption must state on the balance sheet that:

- The company is eligible to take advantage of the audit exemption

- They are aware of their obligation to keep proper records and to prepare accounts that give a true and fair view of the company's position

- No holders of 10 per cent or more of any class of the issued share capital have requested an audit.

This is in addition to the usual statement of directors' responsibilities included in the financial statements.

The Accountant's Report

This report must be prepared by a suitably qualified accountant (who need not be a registered auditor).

The reporting accountant must give his or her opinion on three matters:

- Whether the accounts are in agreement with the accounting records

- Whether, having regard only to, and on the basis of, the information contained in the accounting records, the accounts have been drawn up in a manner consistent with the accounting requirements specified in the Companies Act 1985

- Whether the company has satisfied the conditions for exemption from an audit as specified in the regulations.

In the event that the accounts are not in agreement with the accounting records or not drawn up in accordance with the legislation, the reporting accountant must qualify his or her opinion.

The reporting accountant does not perform an audit — that is, no verification of turnover or balance sheet totals is required nor must independent evidence be obtained to support the figures in the financial statements.

Practice Note 13 gives guidance on the application of Auditing Standards to the audit of small companies.

Reporting Standards for the Smaller Company

A new financial reporting standard for smaller entities (FRSSE) was published in November 1997. Entities falling within its scope **may** choose to present financial statements under its requirements or continue to apply existing standards.

The APB identified four areas of possible concern for auditors. Refer to Bulletin 1997/3 (see page 189) for key points.

STATEMENT OF STANDARDS FOR REPORTING ACCOUNTANTS

AUDIT EXEMPTION REPORTS

ISSUED OCTOBER 1994

EFFECTIVE UK ONLY, FOR REPORTS SIGNED
ON OR AFTER 21 DECEMBER 1994

Summary

Sets out the standards required of accountants reporting on accounts of small companies exempted from the statutory audit requirement but whose turnover is in excess of £90,000 and less than £350,000 (except in the case of a charity, where the gross income limit is £250,000).

Note: The exemption limit for small companies (excluding charities) was raised to £350,000 in 1997.

Key Points

The report must be prepared by a suitably qualified accountant (who need not be a registered auditor).

A letter of engagement is necessary.

Prepare and document a work programme.

Direct, supervise and review work done by assistants.

Working papers should evidence work done and record and support the conclusions reached.

Check that the accounts are in agreement with the ac-counting records — if not, qualify the report.

Check that the accounts have been prepared in accor-dance with the accounting requirements specified in sec-tion 249C(6) of the Companies Act 1985 — if not, qualify the report.

If a limitation is put on the scope of the work, qualify the report.

Do not issue a report if the company is not entitled to exemption from the audit or if unable to reach a conclu-sion on this. Notify the directors.

Resign from the engagement if the accounts are mis-leading (and this cannot be dealt with adequately in the report).

Application Notes

All clients in this category must receive a new letter of engagement — otherwise there will be confusion about exactly what work is being undertaken. Ensure that all existing engagement letters are superseded or with-drawn.

Do not carry out an audit — that is, do not look for original documents, independent evidence, bank confir-mations, debtors, confirmations, title deeds etc.

If the reporting accountant has prepared the financial statements, they should be in agreement with the books of account — otherwise check a number of entries from the nominal ledger through to the final accounts.

Check that the company is exempt from audit — that is:

- Balance sheet totals less than £1,400,000

- Turnover less than £350,000 (if a charity, £250,000)

- The company was not at any time during the year:

  ◊ A public company

  ◊ A banking or insurance company

  ◊ Listed under the Insurance Brokers (Registration) Act 1977

  ◊ An authorised person (or appointed representative) under the Financial Services Act 1986

  ◊ An employer association or trade union

  ◊ A member of a group.

- Use a Companies Act checklist.

Set out details of the accounting records.

Ensure that work delegated to assistants is reviewed and supervised (and evidenced).

Ensure that the financial statements include a statement by the directors that:

- The company is entitled to avail of the audit exemption

- The members (or those of them holding 10 per cent or more of the issued share capital) have not requested an audit

- Note the requirements to keep proper records and to prepare accounts giving a true and fair view.

Example of Accountant's Report with Unqualified Opinion

ACCOUNTANT'S REPORT TO THE SHAREHOLDERS ON
THE UNAUDITED ACCOUNTS OF ABC LIMITED

I report on the accounts for the year ended 31 December 1997 set out on pages 3 to 14.

Respective Responsibilities of Directors and Reporting Accountant:
As described on page 2, the company's directors are responsible for the preparation of the accounts, and they consider that the company is exempt from an audit. It is my responsibility to carry out procedures to enable me to report my opinion.

Basis of Opinion:
My work was conducted in accordance with the Statement of Standards for Reporting Accountants and so my procedures consisted of comparing the accounts with the accounting records kept by the company, and making such limited enquiries of the officers of the company as I considered necessary for the purposes of this report. These procedures provide only the assurance expressed in my opinion.

Opinion:
In my opinion;

(a) The accounts are in agreement with those accounting records kept by the company under section 221 of the Companies Act 1985

(b) Having regard only to, and on the basis of, the information contained in those accounting records,

(i)   the accounts have been drawn up in a manner consistent with the accounting requirements specified in section 249C(6) of the Act, and

(ii) the company satisfied the conditions for exemption from an audit of the accounts for the year specified in section 249A(4) of the Act and did not, at any time within the year, fall within any of the categories of companies not entitled to the exemption specified in section 249B(1).

U NO WHO
Reporting Accountant
Blank Street
1 March 1998

From the example, the following requirements are evident:

- Name(s) of those to whom it is addressed

- Which statements are being reported on

- Responsibilities of the directors set out

- Basis of the opinion explained

- Opinion given

- Name and signature of the reporting accountant

- Date.

STATEMENTS OF INVESTMENT CIRCULAR REPORTING STANDARDS (SIRs)

Introduction

STATEMENTS OF INVESTMENT CIRCULAR REPORTING STANDARDS (SIRS)

SIRs are concerned with the work of reporting accountants which does not come under the framework of audit
regulation in that some of the reports contain not only
historical information but also forecast financial data.

The topics likely to be covered by SIRs include:

- Reports on historical information in investment cir-
culars
- Letters of comfort
- Profit forecasts and projections
- Working capital reports
- Pro forma profit and loss accounts.

Like SASs, the basic principles of SIRs are mandatory,
though they are quite separate publications.

Reporting accountants complying with the SIRs need
not comply with the requirements of SASs, except where
specific reference is made to an SAS.

SIR 100

INVESTMENT CIRCULARS AND REPORTING ACCOUNTANTS

ISSUED DECEMBER 1997

EFFECTIVE FOR ALL REPORTS, LETTERS AND STATEMENTS
SIGNED ON OR AFTER 1 APRIL 1998

Summary

Outlines the general principles and procedures for the
work of the reporting accountant in all engagements
dealing with investment circulars such as prospectuses,
listing particulars, circulars to shareholders, etc.

Key Points

The reporting accountant must:

- Have a good knowledge of the legislation/regulations
  governing the documents involved — including the
  Listing Rules, Alternative Investment Market, Public Offers of Securities Regulations, Financial Services Act or City Code

- Comply with the principles set out in the *Auditor's
  Code*

- Issue detailed engagement letter(s) identifying the
  scope of the engagement and which reports are to be
  published and which are private comfort letters. Ensure any changes to the engagement are agreed in
  writing and signed by the client

- Develop and document a plan to identify potential
  problem areas, identify the different areas of the engagement and for review

- Ensure the engagement team possesses the requisite skills and experience — include specialists where appropriate

- Obtain sufficient evidence to support the team's conclusions

- Maintain good working papers

- Issue reports, conforming to the applicable requirements, to the relevant persons as set out in the engagement letter

- Consider other documents with which the report is to be included to ensure nothing is misleading or inconsistent

- Consider events subsequent to the issue of the report and before the completion date of the transaction.

SIR 200

ACCOUNTANTS' REPORTS ON HISTORICAL FINANCIAL INFORMATION IN INVESTMENT CIRCULARS

ISSUED DECEMBER 1997

EFFECTIVE FOR ALL REPORTS, LETTERS AND STATEMENTS
SIGNED ON OR AFTER 1 APRIL 1998

Summary

Outlines the standards required when reporting on historical financial information to be included in investment circulars.

Key Points

Ensure the reporting accountant is independent of the audit engagement partner where a "true and fair" opinion is required.

Present the information in the report in the format prescribed by all applicable requirements including the Listing Rules, Public Offers of Securities Regulations, etc.

The reporting accountant is responsible for the accurate compilation of the information from source documents.

The responsibility of preparing source documents belongs to the directors or officials of the entity being reported on. Obtain acknowledgement of this responsibility, either in a board minute or representation letter.

Present the information on a consistent and comparable basis.

Only make adjustments to the source documents if required for:

- Consistency

- Comparability

- Highlighting matters of importance

- Correction of material errors.

Obtain agreement for the adjustments with those responsible for issuing the document.

Obtain sufficient knowledge of the entity's business — the financial, economic and market environment in which the business is operating and the viewpoint of the management of the business.

Review the historical data. Consider whether a coherent and representative view of the business has been gathered and obtain sufficient evidence to support conclusions reached thereon.

The reporting accountant should come to an independent judgement on the usefulness and validity of working papers when given access to the auditor's files.

Meet with senior officials of the entity, visit the plant, examine internal controls, analyse the accounts.

Apply SAS 150 *Subsequent Events*, when dealing with the period since the last balance sheet date to the date of the accountants' report.

Joint reporting accountants must rely on each other's working papers — which must therefore be reviewed by the other — as both are jointly and severally responsible for the entire report. This joint responsibility should be acknowledged in writing (joint letter of engagement).

Include in the report a statement of responsibilities for:

- Preparing the report (the reporting accountants)
- The source documents
- The investment circular itself.

Apply the principles of SAS 600 in explaining the basis of the opinion and the clear expression of same in their report.

Indicate how previously qualified audit reports (if applicable) have been resolved.

PRACTICE NOTES
(AT 1 JANUARY 1998)

Introduction

PRACTICE NOTES

The purpose of Practice Notes (PNs) is to give guidance
to auditors on applying the Statements of Auditing
Standards, or one of them, in particular circumstances
or to a particular industry/sector.

PNs are supplementary to, and should be read in conjunction with, SASs.

Many of the practice notes refer to legal or statutory requirements and are not of general interest to students or
most practitioners. Therefore, only a brief overview is
included in this book. One exception is the PN on the
audit of small businesses which is likely to be of more
general interest and for which a longer summary is included.

It is important to note that a detailed knowledge (see
SAS 120) of the applicable PN is required for auditors of
businesses specifically covered by a Practice Note.

Also included in the relevant PNs is the impact of the
1996 regulations extending the statutory duty to report
to regulators.

PRACTICE NOTE 1
INVESTMENT BUSINESSES

ISSUED SEPTEMBER 1992

Summary

Establishes standards and gives guidance to auditors of investment businesses authorised under the Financial Services Act 1986 in relation to client assets, conduct of business rules, audit report to regulators and correspondence with regulators.

Key Points

This PN should be read in conjunction with SAS 620 *The auditor's right and duty to report to regulators in the financial sector.*

Anyone carrying on investment business in the UK must be authorised to do so by one (or more) of the regulatory bodies established under the Financial Services Act 1986.

Investor protection is the primary concern of the regulators and is achieved by ensuring that:

- The firm is financially healthy

- Clients' money and investments are held separately from the firm's own assets in a fiduciary capacity

- The firm acts honestly, promptly, carefully and that its staff are capable.

Compliance with the rules of the regulatory body is monitored:

- By the firm itself:
  - ◊ Using internal quality checks
  - ◊ Sending regular reports to the regulator
- By the regulator in monitoring and inspecting the business
- By the firm's auditor in sending an annual report to the regulator concerning:
  - ◊ Financial statements
  - ◊ Compliance with the regulator's requirements for financial stability
  - ◊ Accounting records and control systems
  - ◊ Client assets.

PRACTICE NOTE 2

THE LLOYD'S MARKET

ISSUED JULY 1992

Summary

Gives guidance to auditors in applying auditing standards to the audit of individuals and entities regulated by the Council of Lloyd's, whose responsibility is the supervision of the affairs of Lloyd's Names and of entities trading in the Lloyd's market.

Key Points

Auditors must comply with the regulations, etc. issued by Lloyd's and update their knowledge regularly due to the continuous changes in regulations.

Auditors' duties under the Lloyd's Act include:

• Reporting to individual underwriting members (Names) of syndicates on financial and other statements. This includes issuing an opinion as to whether the financial statements have been prepared in accordance with the syndicate accounting rules and, for closed years of account, whether a true and fair view of the profit or loss is shown

• Reporting on returns made to Lloyd's Council

• Reporting on financial statements of underwriting agents and brokers.

Materiality must be assessed in terms of the effect on each Name in a syndicate.

A three year basis of accounting is normally used for syndicate accounts. When a year is being closed, a reinsurance charge will be made by the underwriter and the audit of this estimate will normally create the greatest difficulty for the auditor.

Where significant uncertainties remain for a year of account, the managing agent may consider that the year in question remain open until the uncertainties are resolved sufficiently to allow a fair reinsurance premium to be calculated.

Auditors are not required to give a "true and fair" report on accounts for open years of account.

PRACTICE NOTE 3
THE AUDITOR'S RIGHT AND DUTY TO REPORT TO THE BANK OF ENGLAND

ISSUED MARCH 1994

Summary

Gives guidance to auditors and reporting accountants of authorised institutions in applying SAS 620 when considering reporting to the Bank of England.

Key Points

Auditors must be sufficiently knowledgeable to be able to recognise actual or possible breaches of the Banking Act 1987 authorisation criteria and other relevant documents.

Section 47 of the Act — which allows reports to be made to the Bank without contravening any duty (for example, confidentiality) to the client — only protects auditors and reporting accountants where:

- They become aware of the matter being reported on in their capacity as auditors/reporting accountants to the financial institution

- The report is made in good faith — obtain legal advice before making a direct report.

There is a legal duty to report where there is reasonable cause to believe that any of the criteria listed have not been fulfilled **and** this is material to the exercise of the Bank of England's functions.

The criteria include:

- The directors, controllers and managers should be fit and proper persons

- The business should be directed by at least two individuals

- The number of non-executive directors is considered appropriate

- The business is conducted in a prudent manner

- The minimum net assets level is exceeded.

Information given by the Bank of England to auditors/reporting accountants is confidential and should not be disclosed to the client institution.

Note: Since 1996, auditors of an entity closely linked to a regulated entity also have a duty to report matters coming to their attention about the regulated entity in the course of the audit of the closely-linked entity.

PRACTICE NOTE 4

THE AUDITOR'S RIGHT AND DUTY TO REPORT TO THE BUILDING SOCIETIES COMMISSION

ISSUED MARCH 1994

Summary

Gives guidance to auditors of building societies in applying SAS 620 when considering reporting to the Building Societies Commission.

Key Points

The statutory duty to report only applies to the auditors of — not to any reporting accountants involved with — the building society.

Reports to the Commission by auditors come under three headings:

• **An annual systems report**: on compliance with system and control requirements

• **A statutory "right to report"**: on matters considered prejudicial to investments of shareholders or depositors

• **A statutory "duty to report"**: on breaches (actual or possible) of the criteria on prudent management.

Auditors should only use the "right to report" in exceptional circumstances — where there is an actual or potential risk to the investments of members.

The statutory "duty to report" will arise if any criteria of prudent management set out is not satisfactory (actual or perceived) and the auditor has reasonable cause to believe it may be of material significance to the Commission's functions.

The criteria include:

- Maintenance of adequate reserves
- Maintenance of a structure of commercial assets satisfying the legal requirements
- Maintenance of adequate assets in liquid form
- Maintenance of arrangements for assessing the adequacy of securities for advances secured on land
- Maintenance of the requisite accounting records and systems of control of business and of inspection and report
- Conduct of the business with adequate professional skills.

Any failure to meet any of the first five criteria above is automatically a breach of the sixth criteria — for the directors to conduct the business prudently and with integrity (therefore, there is a statutory duty on auditors to report).

Note: Since 1996, auditors of an entity closely linked to a regulated entity also have a duty to report matters coming to their attention about the regulated entity in the course of the audit of the closely-linked entity.

PRACTICE NOTE 5

THE AUDITOR'S RIGHT AND DUTY TO REPORT TO SIB AND OTHER REGULATORS OF INVESTMENT BUSINESSES

ISSUED MARCH 1994

Summary

Gives guidance to auditors and independent accountants of investment businesses in applying SAS 620 when considering reporting to the relevant Financial Services Act regulator.

Key Points

The SIB is responsible for the supervision of regulated entities in order to protect investors.

The auditor's right to report to SIB is not restricted to information concerning the client. It could include customers of the entity, its associated or group companies, an appointed representative or nominee companies. The information must have come to the auditor's notice in their capacity as auditor.

The auditor is protected from a breach of duty claim provided the report is made in good faith and relates to information obtained in their capacity as auditor.

The statutory duty to report applies when matters of significance arise concerned with assessing:

- Whether a person is a fit and proper person to carry on investment business, or

- Whether action should be taken to protect investors from a significant risk of loss, including:

  ◊ A loss of clients' assets

  ◊ Concerns about the financial position of the entity

  ◊ Non-compliance with requirements for the orderly management of its, or its clients', affairs.

Note: Since 1996, auditors of an entity closely linked to a regulated entity also have a duty to report matters coming to their attention about the regulated entity in the course of the audit of the closely-linked entity.

Note: In 1997 the Securities and Investments Board changed its name to the Financial Services Authority and, over the next two years, will acquire the powers and activities of the other eight Self Regulatory Organisations, which it previously regulated. In addition, the Bank of England Bill, expected to be passed in early 1998, will transfer responsibility for supervising banks, wholesale money market institutions and foreign exchange clearing houses from the Bank of England to the Financial Services Authority.

PRACTICE NOTE 6

THE AUDITOR'S RIGHT AND DUTY TO REPORT TO THE DTI IN RELATION TO INSURERS AUTHORISED UNDER THE INSURANCE COMPANIES ACT 1982

ISSUED JULY 1994

Summary

Gives guidance to auditors of entities authorised under the Insurance Companies Act in applying SAS 620 when considering reporting to the UK Department of Trade and Industry.

Key Points

The powers of the DTI are wide and include authorisation of an insurer to carry on insurance business, monitoring of the business and intervention in the affairs of the insurer.

The duty or right to report is not restricted to information concerning the insurer itself which has come to notice in their capacity as auditor. It could include information about the reinsurer of the insurer.

The auditor is protected from a breach of duty claim provided the report is made in good faith and relates to information obtained in their capacity as auditor.

The statutory duty to report arises when matters of significance arise concerning areas such as:

• The minimum margin of solvency has been breached

- The entity's assets are not appropriate for the type of business

- Computation of liabilities are not in accordance with regulations

- There is a potential risk of the insurer not meeting its liabilities

- Writing of unauthorised new business

- Decisions being made without due regard for sound and prudent management

- A failure to notify the DTI of a change in director

- A failure to fulfil any obligation under the Act.

Note: Since 1996, auditors of an entity closely linked to a regulated entity also have a duty to report matters coming to their attention about the regulated entity in the course of the audit of the closely-linked entity.

PRACTICE NOTE 7

THE AUDITOR'S RIGHT AND DUTY TO REPORT TO THE FRIENDLY SOCIETIES COMMISSION

ISSUED JULY 1994

Summary

Gives guidance to auditors of friendly societies in applying SAS 620 when considering reporting to the Friendly Societies Commission.

Key Points

The statutory duty to report only applies to the auditors of — not to any reporting accountants involved with — the friendly society.

Reports to the Commission by auditors come under three headings:

- **An annual systems report**: on (a) compliance with accounting records, (b) system of control and (c) system of inspection and report.

- **A statutory "right to report"**: on matters considered prejudicial to the interests of the society's members.

- **A statutory "duty to report"**: on breaches (actual or possible) of the criteria on prudent management.

Auditors should only use the right to report in exceptional circumstances. In most situations, the matter will also give rise to a duty to report.

The statutory "duty to report" will arise if any criteria of prudent management set out is not satisfactory (actual or perceived) and the auditor has reasonable cause to believe that it may be of material significance to the Commission's functions.

The criteria include:

- Maintenance of adequate reserves

- Maintenance of adequate assets in liquid form

- Maintenance of the requisite accounting records and systems of control of business and of inspection and report

- Conduct of the business with adequate professional skills

- Supervision of subsidiaries and jointly controlled companies.

Any failure to meet any of the first three criteria automatically is a breach of the fourth criteria — for the Committee of Management to conduct the business prudently and with integrity (therefore, there is a statutory duty on the auditor to report).

Note: Since 1996, auditors of an entity closely linked to a regulated entity also have a duty to report matters coming to their attention about the regulated entity in the course of the audit of the closely-linked entity.

PRACTICE NOTE 8

REPORTS BY AUDITORS UNDER COMPANY LEGISLATION IN THE UNITED KINGDOM

ISSUED AUGUST 1994

Summary

Gives guidance on good practice for auditors who need to report on financial statements, revised financial statements, abbreviated accounts, summary financial statements, ceasing to hold office etc.

Key Points

Auditors have a statutory duty under the Companies Act 1985 to report to the members of a company on all financial statements laid before the company in general meeting while holding office.

The duty requires a statement that, in their opinion, the financial statements have been properly prepared in accordance with the Act — and all regulations to be construed as one with that Act (for example, EU regulations) — and whether a true and fair view is given of the:

- State of affairs at the end of the financial year

- Profit or loss for the financial year.

Auditors must not sign their report before the financial statements have been approved by the Board and the balance sheet has been signed by a director on behalf of the Board.

There is a statutory duty to alter the wording in the audit report if:

- The information in the directors' report is not consistent with the financial statements

- Proper accounting records have not been kept

- The financial statements are not in agreement with the accounting records

- The auditors are unable to obtain all the information and explanations considered necessary

- The directors' emoluments and benefits do not comply with the requirements of Schedule 6 of the 1985 Act.

Revised annual financial statements (for example, correction of errors in the original financial statements) or directors' report must be prepared as if prepared at the date of the original financial statements or directors' report. The auditor's opinion is dated as the original report and includes an opinion on whether the original financial statements failed to comply with the Companies Act 1985 in the respects identified by the directors.

Abbreviated Accounts

Where a company intends to file abbreviated accounts with the Registrar of Companies and is qualified to do so as a "small" or "medium-sized" company by sections 246, 247 or 248 of the Companies Act 1985, the auditors must issue a special audit report stating that:

- The company is entitled to the exemptions, and

- The abbreviated accounts have been correctly prepared in accordance with the relevant provisions.

The original report on the full accounts need not be attached to the accounts being filed — unless it was qualified.

Note: This amendment to the filing of abbreviated accounts is effective from April 1997. See Bulletin number 1997/1.

Ceasing to Hold Office

Auditors ceasing to hold office — whether as a result of resignation, removal by the directors or a decision not to stand for reappointment — must send a statement to the company's registered office stating whether there are any circumstances which they consider should be brought to the attention of the members.

If such circumstances exist then, in addition to listing them to the company, the auditors must send a copy to the Registrar of Companies within 28 days (subject to the company applying for a court order against this).

Practice Note 9

Reports by Auditors under Company Legislation in the Republic of Ireland

Issued August 1994

Summary

Gives guidance on good practice for auditors who need to report on financial statements, revised financial statements, abbreviated accounts, summary financial statements, ceasing to hold office etc.

Key Points

Auditors have a statutory duty under the Companies Acts to report to the members of a company on all financial statements laid before the company in general meeting while holding office.

The duty requires a statement whether, in their opinion:

- A true and fair view is given of the:

    ◊ State of affairs as at the end of the financial year

    ◊ Profit or loss for the financial year

- The financial statements have been properly prepared in accordance with the Companies Acts 1963 to 1990, Companies (Amendment) Act 1983 and the European Communities (Companies: Group Accounts) Regulations 1992

- Proper books of account have been kept

- Proper returns have been received from branches not visited by the auditors

- There exists at the balance sheet date a financial situation in the context of Section 40 of the 1983 Act (net assets are half or less of the called up share capital) which may require the convening of an Extraordinary General Meeting

- The information given by the directors' report is consistent with the financial statements

- The balance sheet and profit and loss account are in agreement with the books of account

- The auditors have obtained all the information and explanations necessary for the purposes of their audit.

Auditors must not sign their report before the financial statements have been approved by the Board and both the balance sheet and profit and loss account have been signed by two directors on behalf of the Board.

Abridged Financial Statements

Where a company intends to file abridged financial statements with the Registrar of Companies and is qualified to do so as a "small" or "medium-sized" company by sections 10 to 12 of the Companies Act 1986, the auditors must provide the directors with a report stating that:

- The company is entitled to annex the abridged accounts to the annual return, and

- The abridged accounts have been properly prepared [s18].

A special audit report — in addition to the original report on the full accounts — must be attached to the accounts being filed and a copy of the report given to the directors under s18. The accounts being filed must also include a declaration, signed by the company secretary and a director, that the company is entitled to file abridged financial statements.

"Proper Books of Account" Report

Auditors are obliged to notify the company where they form an opinion that the company is failing to keep "proper books of account" as required by s202 of the 1990 Act and notify the Registrar of Companies within seven days of notifying the company *unless* the company takes steps to ensure that proper books of account are kept.

This report is only required where there are major or material contraventions involved.

Ceasing to Hold Office

Auditors ceasing to hold office — whether as a result of resignation, removal by the directors or a decision not to stand for reappointment — must send a statement to the company's registered office stating there are no circumstances which they consider should be brought to the attention of the members or creditors.

If such circumstances exist, these should be listed. In addition to listing them to the company, the auditors must send a copy of the listing to the Registrar of Companies within 14 days.

Where "particular circumstances" are notified to the company, the company must:

- Circulate copies to all those entitled to receive the financial statements

- Convene a general meeting, if requested by the resigning auditor.

PRACTICE NOTE 10

AUDIT OF CENTRAL GOVERNMENT FINANCIAL STATEMENTS IN THE UNITED KINGDOM

ISSUED FEBRUARY 1996

Summary

Gives guidance to auditors on the application of SASs to audits in the central government sector (government departments, public bodies, etc.). The Practice Note does not apply to local authorities, health authorities or nationalised industries.

Key Points

The central government sector has many different funding and financial reporting arrangements. The auditor must have knowledge of those arrangements relating to the body being audited.

Audits of public sector bodies often have a specific duty, set out in the letter of appointment, to examine and report on the compliance of transactions with the law, regulations, Parliamentary or Treasury authority (concept of **regularity**).

Auditors must also have regard to the concept of **propriety** (high standards of conduct, behaviour and corporate governance are expected in public business), though this is not expressly covered in the opinion on the financial statements. Examples of matters to be considered include:

- Equal opportunities for job vacancies
- Avoidance from personal profit from public business
- Ensuring open competition for contracts, etc.

PRACTICE NOTE 11

THE AUDIT OF CHARITIES

ISSUED OCTOBER 1996

Summary

Gives guidance to auditors on the application of SASs to audits of charities and in applying the requirements of the Charities (Accounts and Reports) Regulations to unincorporated charities.

Key Points

The duty to report to the Charity Commission arises when the auditor becomes aware of information likely to be of material significance to the Charity Commission in exercising its powers to commence enquiries or protect charities, including where:

- Inadequate arrangements are in place for managing the affairs of the charity

- There has been a material breach of the trust or other legislation

- There has probably been a misuse of the assets.

The accounting and reporting rules differ between charities with various income, expenditure levels — although proper accounting records are a necessity for all charities.

The governing document of each charity is likely to be unique and may require the auditor to extend the scope of the audit beyond the statutory requirements.

The accounts of charities subject to audit should, except in rare cases, follow the guidance given in the Statement of Recommended Practice *Accounting by Charities*. For example, money received for specific purposes (restricted funds) must be separately disclosed in the accounts and cannot be used for general purposes without breaching the duty of trust.

Auditors ceasing to hold office, for whatever reason, should issue a statement to the Trustees, with a copy to the Charity Commission, indicating whether there are any matters in relation to the cessation which should be brought to the attention of the Trustees.

Note: Since 1996, auditors of an entity closely linked to a regulated entity also have a duty to report matters coming to their attention about the regulated entity in the course of the audit of the closely-linked entity.

Practice Note 12
Money Laundering

Issued May 1997

Summary

Gives guidance to auditors on their responsibilities where they come across situations where the proceeds of crime are changed so as to appear as legitimate sources of income.

Key Points

Auditors of entities carrying out "relevant financial business", including insurance, banking, credit union or investment businesses:

- May have a statutory duty to report to a regulator.

- May be required to report to a regulator on compliance with Money Laundering Regulations 1993 (UK) in addition to the audit.

Auditors of entities in the public sector:

- Normally will be required to report (this will be set out in the letter of appointment) on compliance of transactions with the law, regulations, Parliamentary or Treasury authority

- Must have regard to the concept of propriety (high standards of conduct, behaviour and corporate governance are expected in public business). Money laundering will therefore be reportable.

Auditors of other entities:

- Have no specific reporting responsibilities except where the entity is governed by regulations (for example, charities)

- Must assess the situation, where information is discovered during the audit to suggest the possibility of money laundering, consider the effects on the financial statements and the implications for other aspects of the audit

- Have a legal duty to report knowledge or suspicions in relation to money laundering of the proceeds of drugs or terrorism.

PRACTICE NOTE 13

THE AUDIT OF SMALL BUSINESSES

ISSUED JULY 1997

Summary

Gives guidance on the application of SASs to the audit of businesses where there is a concentration of ownership and management in a small number of persons (often one) and where there are few sources of income, uncomplicated activities, simple record keeping or limited internal controls.

Key Points

SASs apply to all audits. Special considerations which apply to small businesses are listed below.

SAS 110 Fraud and error
The risk level may increase for instance where:

- The owner manager has a specific motive to distort the financial statements

- No distinction is made between business and personal transactions

- The lifestyle of the owner/manager is inconsistent with their level of remuneration

- Limitations are placed on the scope of the audit

- There is a significant level of cash takings without adequate documentation

- Some of the detailed accounting records are unavailable

- There exists a weak system of internal controls (for example, lack of segregation of duties)

- Significant differences arise between the accounting records and third party confirmations.

Note: Many of the above also apply to audits of larger businesses — see Application Notes to SAS 110.

SAS 120 Consideration of law and regulations
The major impact on small businesses will be companies legislation requirements relating to financial statements preparation and filing.

Some small businesses may also be subject to industry specific legislation/regulation — for example, public houses, restaurants, betting shops etc.

SAS 130 The going concern basis in financial statements
Detailed budgets and forecasts will not be available in most small businesses.

Where a major assumption is critical in the assessment of going concern, it may be necessary to obtain a written representation from the owner/manager confirming the evidence/discussions. Refer to Appendix 2 of the SAS itself for practical advice.

But do not rely solely on the owner/manager's written confirmation — the auditor must comply with the requirements of the SAS.

SAS 140 Engagement letters
An up-to-date engagement letter is very important when dealing with owner/managers. Set out and distinguish between the legal responsibilities of the owner/manager and the auditors in relation to the audit and the other

services provided. Stress that the owner/manager(s), as director(s), are responsible for the financial statements even where the auditor has helped to prepare them (perhaps as part of an accountancy service also provided).

SAS 150 Subsequent events
This procedure normally covers a long period in the case of small businesses.

Where records have not been written up in detail since the year end, inspect/review bank statements, VAT returns, etc. to ascertain whether any adjustments to the financial statements are required.

SAS 160 Other information in documents containing audited information
It is generally easy to comply with this SAS as the auditor will often be involved in assisting the owner/manager in preparing the directors' report and any other information to be included with the financial statements.

SAS 200 Planning
Consider the potential for management over-ride of internal controls in assessing audit risk and in planning the audit.

Plan accountancy services to ensure appropriate audit evidence is obtained suitable for audit purposes.

When the audit for one year is complete, prepare a file note highlighting the major issues encountered that could affect the next year's audit planning.

SAS 210 Knowledge of the business
The auditors' knowledge of the small business must be documented. Normally fairly brief highlights of topics such as: the activities undertaken; tax records; accounting records; management style; summary of profitability; cash flow; related parties (where applicable) will be sufficient.

(See the suggested contents of a permanent audit file in the Application Notes to SAS 210.)

SAS 220 Materiality and the audit
Be careful in applying a quantitative rule of thumb for materiality — for example, five per cent of profits — where the results of the business are near "break-even". Too low a figure will lead to high audit testing. Consider selecting a percentage of turnover or balance sheet totals or previous years' profits.

Assessment of materiality will be easier if draft accounts have been prepared. Consider using different levels of materiality for different aspects of the accounts.

SAS 230 Working papers
These must show the objective; the work performed; the evidence collected and the conclusions reached.

This also applies to "accountancy work" which was planned to be used for audit purposes. Working papers will naturally be less complex than for large businesses but they must show, where necessary, evidence of review by the engagement partner.

SAS 240 Quality control for audit work
In many instances, the audit engagement partner is the only person involved in the audit of the small business

and the requirements of SAS 240 regarding training, assigning and delegating of staff, review, etc. does not apply.

Ensure working papers record all the important items.

The requirement for the firm to have quality control policies (as per SAS 240) applies.

SAS 300 Accounting and internal control systems and audit risk assessments
In many instances, the involvement of the auditor's bookkeeping service in the preparation of the financial statements often can lead to a lower assessment of the level of inherent risk.

Assess the material financial statement assertions carefully to keep audit work to the minimum.

Document briefly the factors which the auditor feels reduces the level of inherent risk from an assumed high level.

Audit evidence obtained through substantive tests will often be the norm in small businesses, together with the work undertaken in preparing the financial statements.

SAS 400 Audit evidence
Plan accountancy work with the needs of the audit in mind and ensure that, where possible, the work is reviewed by another staff member.

Tests of internal control, where available, can allow a reduction in the level of substantive testing.

Substantive testing will be necessary where there are no controls over the completeness of important items. This may include:

- A reconciliation of goods despatched or time sheets to sales invoices

- A review of transactions after the balance sheet date

- Analytical procedures.

SAS 410 Analytical procedures
Analytical procedures for planning the audit will be most effective where the bookkeeping service is complete and financial statements prepared with analyses of various items of income and expenditure is available.

Using analytical procedures as substantive procedures can often be a very cost-effective means of obtaining audit evidence — for example:

- Total payroll cost can be easily corroborated where there is a stable level of staff with little overtime

- The reasonableness of financial statement assertions can be supported in cases where trade ratios can be used.

Analytical procedures to be used as part of the overall review stage of the audit will, for many small businesses, comprise of:

- Comparing the present year's financial statements with previous years'

- Reviewing the trends in financial ratios

- Obtaining explanations of any unexpected features in either the review or the comparison

- Considering whether changes (if any) in the business are reflected in the financial statements

- Comparing the results with budgets or management expectations (not always available).

SAS 420 Audit of accounting estimates
In preparation of the accounts (quite common), the auditor will normally have been involved with the owner/manager in determining the amounts of the estimates to be included in the financial statements. Notes should be taken for the audit file of how the estimates were determined.

Knowledge and experience gained from previous audits (for example, the actual outcome of previous estimates) will assist in assessing whether the risk of error in the estimates is high or not.

SAS 430 Audit sampling
Often the auditor will find that, due to the small populations encountered, it is often easier to test 100 per cent of a population or 100 per cent of key items in the population than to ascertain sampling risk, errors acceptable and selection of representative samples.

SAS 440 Management representations
Representations from the owner/manager on key areas — for example, completeness of liabilities or income — must be assessed in conjunction with other audit procedures. If other audit evidence cannot be obtained, consider whether this puts a limitation on the scope of the audit.

SAS 450 Opening balances and comparatives
This will only apply when the limited company has taken advantage of the UK exemption from audit for small companies.

Auditors need to obtain sufficient evidence regarding the opening balances and comparatives. If unable to do so, consider the implications for the report.

SAS 460 Related parties
Involvement with the preparation of financial statements, knowledge of the business (the people, sources of income and expenditure, accounting records), tax advice and returns will often allow the auditor to assess the risk of related party transactions.

Where related party transactions exist, it is often easy to examine all items as the accounting population is normally small.

As part of the audit planning stage, the auditor should ensure that details of related party transactions are highlighted during the performance of the bookkeeping service.

SAS 470 Overall review of financial statements
Where the accounts have been prepared by the auditors, they should be compared to a checklist of items to be disclosed. This will reduce the work necessary to comply with the SAS.

As with the large businesses, consider whether the financial statements have been unduly influenced by the owner/manager's desire to present matters in a favourable or unfavourable light (for example, to make the bank balance look better, to reduce the tax bill, etc.).

SAS 500 Considering the work of internal audit
Unlikely to apply, as there is seldom an internal audit
function in small businesses.

*SAS 510 The relationship between principal auditors
and other auditors*
Unlikely to apply in the case of small businesses.

SAS 520 Using the work of an expert
The most likely areas where this applies are:

- Using an actuary to value the pension scheme

- Obtaining legal advice on litigation

- Property valuation.

SAS 600 Auditors' reports on financial statements
Where a small company is entitled to, and avails of, the
exemptions under the 1985 UK Act regarding abridged
accounts which, in all other respects, give a true and fair
view, do not qualify the audit opinion.

Other than the above situation, where the financial
statements do not give a true and fair view, the auditor
should qualify his opinion as required by SAS 600.

Auditors should sign their report as soon as possible after the date on which the financial statements are approved by the directors (preferably the same day).
Where there is a delay, ensure that no subsequent
events have occurred between the directors' approval of
the accounts and the signing of the audit report.

SAS 610 Report to directors or management
Prepare a file note of weaknesses identified and discussed with management and use this as part of the re-

quirements of SAS 210 in obtaining knowledge of the
business and SAS 200 in planning future audits.

*SAS 620 The auditor's right and duty to report to regula-
tors in the financial sector*
This SAS only applies where there is a duty to report
direct to the regulator, for example:

- Businesses carrying on investment business

- Unincorporated charities in England and Wales

- Occupational pension schemes.

Only auditors with clients in the above category need to
know SAS 620 in detail (and the relevant Practice Note
where applicable).

PRACTICE NOTE 14
THE AUDIT OF REGISTERED SOCIAL LANDLORDS IN THE UNITED KINGDOM

ISSUED SEPTEMBER 1997

Summary

Gives guidance to auditors in applying auditing standards to the audit of registered social landlords (RSLs) in the United Kingdom.

Key Points

RSLs can operate in different forms of legal entities and the auditor must have knowledge of the particular regulations applicable, including codes of audit practice issued by the regulatory body. Where registered as a charity, Practice Note 11 also applies.

In addition to the normal audit report, the auditor must report if proper controls over transactions of the RSL have not been kept.

Financial statements will usually be drawn up in accordance with the Statement of Recommended Practice developed for housing associations.

Corporation tax and VAT are likely to be complicated areas for many associations.

There is no statutory duty to report to regulators, except in the case of unincorporated charities.

PRACTICE NOTE 15

THE AUDIT OF OCCUPATIONAL PENSION SCHEMES IN THE UNITED KINGDOM

ISSUED NOVEMBER 1997

Summary

Gives guidance to auditors in applying SAS 620 when considering reporting to the Occupational Pensions Regulatory Body (OPRA) and sets out the special considerations in applying auditing standards to the audit of occupational pension schemes.

Key Points

The auditor must have detailed knowledge of the trust deed (or other document establishing the scheme rules).

Except in rare cases, the financial statements should be prepared in accordance with the Statement of Recommended Practice *Financial reports of pension schemes*.

In the case of a defined benefit scheme, the auditors' report does not give an opinion on the true and fair view of the state of affairs of the scheme but rather of the scheme's financial assets and transactions and liabilities other than liabilities to pay pensions and benefits after the end of the scheme year and confirmation that contributions to the scheme have been paid in accordance with the actuary's recommendations.

There is a statutory duty to report to the regulator (OPRA) matters likely to be significant — for example, failure to meet contribution schedules, fraud (actual or suspected), possible money laundering, a qualified audit opinion or material failures in administering the scheme. Report even where the trustees or actuaries have already reported.

Ensure the letter of engagement from the trustees authorises the auditor to communicate with the scheme actuary, the administrator, sponsoring employer etc. where third parties have provided services to the trustees.

Investments often form the principal asset of a pension scheme and the income from investments form a key element in ensuring the scheme can meet its future obligations. Where trustees have appointed an investment manager on behalf of the scheme, consider the controls operated by the trustees over the services provided.

Note: Since 1996, auditors of an entity closely linked to a regulated entity also have a duty to report matters coming to their attention about the regulated entity in the course of the audit of the closely-linked entity.

BULLETINS

AT 1 JANUARY 1998

BULLETIN 1993/1

REVIEW OF INTERIM FINANCIAL INFORMATION

Summary

This bulletin provides guidance to auditors in reviewing and reporting on interim financial information produced by listed companies complying with the requirements of the London Stock Exchange.

Key Points

The auditor's review report gives a level of assurance significantly below that of an audit opinion due to the limited scope of the review.

Agree an engagement letter setting out the key terms of the review.

Establish the review work required, if any, on each subsidiary and division, assessing the potential risk of error on the consolidated interim information.

Discuss the results of the review with the audit committee and board of directors.

The review report states:

* That accounting policies consistent with the previous full year's financial statements have been used, and

* Whether any material modifications to the information should be made.

Ensure that readers note that an audit opinion is not expressed.

Application Notes

Plan the work and use staff with requisite skills and experience.

Update knowledge of financial, economic and market environment of the business. Discuss with key management.

Consider whether the information gathered from the different sources (for example, management, group/subsidiary/divisional level, economic data, etc.) presents a coherent and representative view of the interim results.

BULLETIN 1995/1

DISCLOSURES RELATING TO CORPORATE GOVERNANCE (REVISED)

Summary

Provides guidance to auditors when reporting on a company's compliance with the *Code of best practice* specified by the London Stock Exchange, arising from the report of the Committee on the Financial Aspects of Corporate Governance (the "Cadbury Report").

Key Points

The Stock Exchange requires that each company must state, in the annual report, whether it has complied with the *Code of best practice* during the year and give details of any non-compliance.

The auditor must review the company's statement of compliance insofar as it relates to the following:

- The board of directors has a formal schedule of matters specifically reserved to it for decision
- There is an agreed procedure for directors to take independent advice, at the company's expense, in relation to their duties
- Non-executive directors should be appointed for specific terms and re-appointment should not be automatic
- The appointment and selection of non-executive directors should be a matter for the entire board
- An audit committee should be established (of at least three non-executive directors).

- A statement of directors' responsibilities for preparing the accounts should be placed near the auditor's statement of their reporting responsibilities

- The directors should report on the effectiveness of the system of internal control (guidance on this aspect was published in December 1994).

Note: A number of other requirements were replaced by Bulletin 1996/3 and Bulletin 1997/2.

Agree an engagement letter outlining the scope of the work. Ensure that the directors understand that:

- No assurance on the effectiveness of the system of internal financial control will be expressed, and

- No extra work will be carried out to confirm the business is a going concern (this is now a requirement of the Listing Rules)

and that these points will also be stressed in the review report.

Review the minutes of meetings of the board of directors and committees.

Review supporting documents prepared for the board or any committee relating to the matters of compliance.

Make enquiries of the chairman of the board and committees to ensure the procedures set out in the code are implemented.

Attend meetings of the audit committee when the annual report is being discussed and approved.

BULLETIN 1996/2
THE AUDITORS' RIGHT AND DUTY TO REPORT TO REGULATORS: IMPLEMENTATION OF THE POST-BCCI DIRECTIVE IN THE UK

Summary

Gives guidance to auditors on the changes to the statutory duty to report to regulators and to SAS 620 on the implementation of the Financial Institution (Prudential Supervision) Regulations 1996.

Key Points

No major change to the matters to be considered by auditors when deciding to report.

The statutory duty to report is extended where auditors of an entity closely linked to a regulated entity must report matters coming to their attention about the regulated entity in the course of the audit of the "closely-linked" entity.

BULLETIN 1996/3

DISCLOSURES RELATING TO CORPORATE GOVERNANCE (SUPPLEMENT)

Summary

Updates guidance issued in Bulletin 1995/1, as a result of changes to the Stock Exchange listing rules on going concern, directors' remuneration and the financial aspects of corporate governance.

Key Points

A separate Listing Rule incorporating the *Code of best practice* requirement for a statement by the directors on the entity's going concern status.

The auditor must ensure that:

- The directors' statement on going concern is in accordance with the Listing Rule requirements

- No discrepancy exists between the directors' statement and the information obtained in the course of the audit

- Ensure the review report to the directors stresses that no extra audit work was done to check whether the entity can continue to operate as a going concern and no opinion on the matter is being expressed.

For new Listing Rules requirements relating to disclosure of directors' remuneration, see Bulletin 1997/2.

BULLETIN 1996/4

EQUALISATION RESERVES

Summary

Provides guidance to auditors in issuing audit reports under SAS 600 when reporting on the financial statements of those insurers required by law to establish and maintain equalisation reserves (these relate to a business subject to catastrophe claims).

Key Points

Ensure the equalisation reserve has been calculated in accordance with the formulae set out in either the 1990 or 1996 Regulations (whichever is applicable).

Ensure that equalisation reserves are included in the balance sheet as part of "Technical provisions" (a liability).

Ensure that there is an explanatory note in the financial statements on how the equalisation reserves have been calculated and their effect on the results.

An unqualified audit report is given where the financial statements include the preceding points.

Include in the audit report an additional comment relating to the equalisation reserves and drawing the readers' attention to the disclosure notes.

BULLETIN 1997/1

THE SPECIAL AUDITORS' REPORT ON ABBREVIATED ACCOUNTS IN GREAT BRITAIN[1]

Summary

Gives guidance on the special auditors' report on abbreviated accounts required when filing with the Registrar, resulting from the changes in legislation in 1997 (amends Practice Note 8).

Key Points

A special auditors' report is required to be attached to the abbreviated accounts being filed stating that:

- The company is entitled to the exemptions, and

- The abbreviated accounts have been prepared in accordance with the relevant provisions.

The original report on the full accounts need not be attached to the accounts being filed — unless the original report was qualified.

Do not sign the report until the accounts are approved (and signed) by the directors.

---

[1] Bulletin 1997/1 was issued in response to the provisions of SI 1997 No. 220 for which there are yet no equivalent provisions in Northern Ireland — hence the use of "Great Britain" and not "UK" in the title.

Preferably, abbreviated accounts should be prepared and signed at about the same time as the full statements.

Where a "fundamental uncertainty" was included in the auditors' report on the full financial statements by way of an explanatory note, it should also be included in the special report.

BULLETIN 1997/2

DISCLOSURE OF DIRECTORS' REMUNERATION

Summary

Gives guidance on the UK Listing Rules which expand the scope of the auditors' work and which specify a new reporting requirement for auditors of listed companies. Also includes guidance on revised statutory requirements on disclosure of directors' emoluments.

Key Points

The auditors must ensure that the disclosure of the following items (of the 11 set out in the Listing Rules) complies with the:

- Information on share options for each director in accordance with the Accounting Standards Board's UITF Abstract 10

- Details of long-term incentive schemes for each director

- The amount of each element in the remuneration package for each director or former director (basic salary, benefits in kind, bonuses, any other element)

- Details of pension entitlements for defined benefit schemes

- Amount of the increase during the year

- Transfer value of the accrued benefit or sufficient information to enable an assessment of the transfer value to be made

- Details of company contributions during the year for money purchase schemes.

The auditors must state in their report any non-compliance with the disclosure requirements and give the required particulars, as far as is possible.

Ensure the engagement letter for listed companies includes the expanded scope of the audit regarding disclosure of emoluments.

Non-compliance with the Listing Rules does not, of itself, give rise to a qualified opinion on the financial statements. Show separately in the "Opinion" section of the audit report under the heading "Other matters".

Disclosure of directors' remuneration in the statutory accounts has been changed with effect from 1997. Disclose, for listed companies, the aggregate of:

- Emoluments (salary, fees, bonuses, etc.)

- Gains made on the exercise of share options

- Gains made under long term incentive schemes

- Company contributions to money purchase pension schemes

- The number of directors accruing benefits under money purchase pension schemes

- The number of directors accruing benefits under defined benefit pension schemes

Unlisted companies must show the number of directors who exercised share options and who received or became entitled to shares under long term incentive schemes instead of the "gains" made.

BULLETIN 1997/3

THE FRSSE – GUIDANCE FOR AUDITORS

Summary

Gives guidance to auditors of entities opting to prepare financial statements in accordance with the Financial Reporting Standard for Smaller Entities (FRSSE). Four aspects of the FRSSE are addressed in this Bulletin.

Key Points

Accounting treatment of transaction or event
Where an accounting treatment set out in the FRSSE is followed, do not refer to SSAPs, FRSs or UITF Statements for a possible alternative treatment.

Where an accounting treatment is not set out in the FRSSE (expected to be rare for small entities), follow the treatment provided in the relevant SSAP, FRS or UITF Statement. May have to use "true and fair" override — follow disclosures required by the FRSSE.

Cash Flow Statements
Not mandatory but encouraged, however:

- If omitted — no mention required in auditors' report or financial statements

- If in annual report but outside financial statements — auditors should refer to SAS 160

- If included in the financial statements — auditors' responsibilities similar to any (large) entity including voluntary information.

Related party disclosures (SAS 460)
The FRSSE requires that the materiality of related
party transactions should only be assessed in terms of
the reporting entity — this overrides SAS 460's requirement for smaller entities preparing financial
statements under the FRSSE.

Effect on the audit report
Financial statements must disclose that they have been
prepared in accordance with the FRSSE. Auditors
should include a mention of the FRSSE in the introduc-
tory paragraph of their report —

> "We have audited the financial statements on
> pages 5 to 18 which have been prepared in accor-
> dance with the Financial Reporting Standard for
> Smaller Entities . . ."

OTHER DOCUMENTS

THE AUDIT AGENDA – NEXT STEPS

ISSUED FEBRUARY 1996

Summary

This discussion paper, following from the responses to the 1994 paper *The Audit Agenda*, sets out the future developments in auditing required to meet the APB's overall objectives of establishing high standards of auditing, meeting the developing needs of users of financial statements, and enhancing public confidence in the auditing process.

Key Points

The scope of the audit of smaller owner/managed business should be differentiated from the audit of large complex entities (including those listed on the Stock Exchange).

Guidance on the application of SASs to the smaller business will be developed.

Additional guidance may be required for auditors of listed companies in the application of SAS 160 *Other information in documents containing audited financial information* to avoid association with misleading information.

Closer co-operation is envisaged between external and internal auditors to prevent and detect fraud.

Establishment by APB of a fraud task force to identify factors giving rise to fraud and to review educational requirements for auditors on this topic.

Legal penalties for an entity's officers and directors involved in deceiving the auditors should be increased.

Development of reporting standards for directors to be used in their assessment of "going concern" as part of corporate governance requirements.

Consideration to amending SAS 600 so as to emphasise the role of the partner in the audit firm responsible for the audit.

Consideration that the audit engagement partner should attend the entity's AGM and answer relevant questions.

Development of guidance for audit committees to ensure closer involvement with the external auditors. Consideration that the audit committee chairman report at the AGM on matters relating to the appointment and remuneration of the auditors.

Consideration of the potential exposure of auditors to litigation if the scope of the audit is extended – for example, into corporate governance issues, reporting on internal controls.

Investigation of techniques in which the quality of the audit (at a reasonable cost) can be improved.

APB to develop a programme of research for developing future auditing standards.

THE AUDITORS' CODE

ISSUED FEBRUARY 1996

Summary

This discussion paper outlines the fundamental principles which govern the conduct of independent auditors.

Key Points

Persons dealing with independent auditors expect them
to:

- Be honest and fair

- Keep information confidential (unless public interest
  or the law require otherwise)

- Be objective and independent

- Act on behalf of the primary stakeholders (the
  shareholders, in the case of a company)

- Have a high degree of professionalism (assign appropriate staff, sufficient knowledge and expertise, etc.)

- Be thorough and competent

- Assess correctly what is (or is not) material in each
  case

- Communicate their opinion clearly and in an under-
  standable way

- Ensure that other information included (and therefore associated) with their opinion does not cause
  readers to have doubts as to the accuracy of the
  opinion

- Provide officers of the entity with constructive ideas
  arising out of the audit (to add value to the audit).

INTERNAL FINANCIAL CONTROL EFFECTIVENESS

ISSUED APRIL 1995

Summary

This discussion paper sets out a framework for achieving the recommendation of the Cadbury Report (*Code of good practice*) that directors should make a statement on the effectiveness of the system of internal control.

Key Points

At present, the guidance issued to directors by the working party only requires them to confirm that they have reviewed the system of internal control. No conclusion on its effectiveness is demanded.

The paper suggests that other important issues should be considered in the debate:

- How to help companies improve internal controls

- How to best communicate the auditors' views on internal control to the directors and members.

Directors assess the effectiveness of internal financial control under five criteria:

- The control environment

- Identification and evaluation of risks and control objectives

- Information and communication

- Control procedures

- Directive action.

A number of unsuccessful attempts have been made in the USA to legislate public reporting on internal control effectiveness.

Some of the issues discussed include:

- The meaning of the word "effectiveness"

- Whether the auditor should report on the effectiveness of the directors' review rather than on the effectiveness of the system of internal financial control

- The definition of material weaknesses and how to report same

- Communication of the directors' and auditors' reports on the effectiveness of internal financial control

- The appropriateness of the audit report in dealing with the safeguarding of assets

- The impact of additional work to comply with increased scope of the audit on fees

- The advantages and disadvantages of the auditor giving a positive or a negative assurance

- Extra work involved if the review of internal controls is up to the date of approval of the financial statements

- Advantages or disadvantages of restricting audit liability for the report on internal control effectiveness.